THE LANGUAGE OF SELF-AFFIRMATION

A MAGICAL PRACTICE OF MANIFESTING PERSONAL POWER

Caitlin Santomauro

Library of Congress Cataloging-in-Publication Data
LCCN: 2025911314

EBOOK 978-1-958165-48-5
PAPERBACK 978-1-958165-45-4
HARDBACK 978-1-958165-47-8

Editor: Mary Carpenter
Be Extraordinary Publishing
New York

Table of Contents

Dedication

This creation is for my younger self.
To show her, and all our inner children,
that there is no dream fully lost
and we are worthy of our goals
and aspirations, no matter how "unrealistic" they
may seem.

All things are being created. All is aligned.
All is unfolding.

Introduction: Self–Affirmation

> *May all who stumble upon this book*
> *find true empowerment, love, and*
> *connection to self.*
> With Love, C.M.S.

Self-affirmation (noun)

self-af•fir•ma•tion

: the act of validating one's own worthiness and value as an individual for beneficial effect (such as increasing one's confidence or raising self-esteem)

To all the beautiful readers who have found this book for your own healing purposes, I ask you to come into this space and time, for you and you alone. If you are holding this book, you are like me and you are on your journey to self-healing and growth, discovering the personal power that comes from inside your being. Maybe you're just beginning or perhaps you have been on this journey for quite some time. It does not matter. All that matters is that you are here and you are now.

This work is for all the souls that are on the path towards their life's purpose. Self-affirmation is the link to empower yourself, using your own energetic voice. *It is an inspired practice to manifest potentials into reality*, because words are energy, words have power, and your words can create your desired existence.

The writing between these pages comes directly from my own personal experience with the use of language and positive thinking. It is a guide to awaken the healing powers that come from within. I share my stories of self-discovery in every chapter, hoping that you may find identification and inspiration as you explore your own pathway.

This journey begins with trust and faith. Faith of all kinds, whether religious or spiritual, brings you closer to your dreams. It is the basis of your values and principles, which influence your goals and intentions. It gives you inner strength. It gives you inner peace, and *the secret to manifestation IS the cultivation of inner peace.*

If the word "faith" evokes discomfort, or doesn't resonate with you in any way, I invite you to consider connecting to something, anything, that is bigger than yourself. This can be nature, the universe, or elements such as wind or fire. The practice of "faith" and "trust" is simply the practice of believing that there are forces outside of yourself that are powerful enough to help guide you on your way. *This is the suggestion that if you believe, you can create.*

My own faith is very eclectic and pulls from many different sources of spirituality, religion, philosophy, and ethics. Throughout this book you will hear quotes from diverse experts, presenting you with a variety of ideas, beliefs, and practices, to use at your own discretion.

While observing the different suggestions, take what works for you and if something doesn't resonate, let it be. Arrive here with an open mind and heart. I offer you the space to sit with the questions posed within each section. Take a moment to reflect, respond, and write down any of your own thoughts that may arise during this process. Journaling is such a beautiful therapeutic practice that allows you to see and think more clearly.

Remember, this is for you. The work that is being done is yours, and yours alone. As you go through this practice, move forward without judgment, and without expectation. Just allow it to unfold in the way it's supposed to be.

My hope is that this book will help you connect to your words, your power, and manifest your desired reality. Allow me to take you down the unbeaten path of discovering who the fuck you are and what you are capable of. All you need is a little faith, a journal, pen or pencil, and trust in yourself and your expanding journey.

Section One
"I Am."

Who The F*ck Am I?

Affirmation

I am Soft yet Stable.

I am Kind yet Strong.

*I am Gentle yet Powerful as F*ck.*

Self (noun)

> **a**: an individual's typical character or behavior
> **b**: oneself or itself

I am sure you may be thinking, "who is this chick?" And I get it.

Truthfully, I'm not new to the intrusive thoughts of imposter syndrome. I often ask myself this exact question. So let me tell you who I am. Sharing my story, and the experiences I endured to get to where I am today, is important for you as a reader and also a good reminder for myself, to distinguish how this practice has truly morphed my life.

I am a person who used to live a life consumed with shadow, shame, and spiritual ruin. My early adulthood was filled with confronting past trauma, constant chaos, addiction, and disappointment. After escaping the darkest days of my life, there was so much work to be done and so much healing to occur.

In the healing process I found the power of words. With my words, I was able to develop a relationship with *myself* that has enhanced my life tremendously. I have found that language is the key to shifting energy. Your voice is your power. As I transformed my life from stagnancy to all potential possibilities, I connected to a *magical* practice of affirmations.

I am here to show you that the power of positive thought actually works! I am proof of the practice. When creating this book, I began reviewing all of my past journals. I reflected on the affirmations I wrote and was struck with so much gratitude when I realized that all the things I have focused on manifesting into my life have come to fruition.

Did everything come into existence exactly how I thought it would? Not at all. But it was created nonetheless. I share my experiences so you can see how this practice enabled me to build a life filled with joy, passion, and sovereignty.

The trick to becoming the creator of your world is to fully connect to yourself. Having confidence in yourself. Having love for yourself. And believing in yourself.

In the next few chapters, I will dive deeper into where I was, where I had to go, and where I am today, extending the hope that with the power of positive words, you too can manifest a world filled with happiness, peace and freedom.

Chapter 1: The Past

Affirmation

I free myself from the cage of my past,
accepting all that is & all that has transpired.

I acknowledge growth from my experiences,
moving through challenges to truly embrace who I am.

I let go of self-judgment & regret,
finding the courage to practice forgiveness & self-love.

It is so.

Experience (noun)

ex·pe·ri·ence

    a: direct observation of or participation in events as a basis of knowledge

    b: the fact or state of having been affected by or gained knowledge through direct observation or participation

Throughout my life experience, I have found myself lost in many different ways. From a young age, I never really fit in with the "normal" crowd and constantly felt the need to fit myself into a box of normalcy in order to be accepted. Was this reality or self-deception? I don't think I'll ever really know, but those were my feelings throughout my childhood, teenage years, and into my twenties.

Early on in my life, I figured out how to find *instant gratification* from outside validation. The key words here are *instant* and *outside*. I always needed a quick fix because I didn't know how to process uncomfortable feelings such as sadness, anger, or shame. I couldn't understand how to navigate those emotions, so I needed things, or people, in order to feel safe. I had a lack of patience and zero ability to regulate or find comfort within myself. My self-perception was damaging. I was always judging and comparing myself to others, always feeling less than, and had very little confidence.

To cope, I developed the habit of codependency. It started with validation from family, friends, and men, and grew into experimenting with alcohol and other substances. I was grappling with complex feelings that came from societal norms and familial expectations. I was always *supposed* to be the "good girl." Quiet, soft, homemaker, and perfect, are just some words that come to mind. I didn't feel like any of those things. I was wild and wacky. I was silly and loud. I was weird, for lack of better terms, which in the most beautifully ironic way, is something I am proud of today. But, it took me thirty years to get here.

The problem was that the feelings of inadequacy, or "being the misfit," became habitual. Solid thought patterns once ingrained in the mind, govern the way you move in all areas of your life, and are very hard to reroute. To quote my girl Taylor Swift (Yes, I am a Swifty), "Old habits die screaming." Once a habit is formed, the human brain will continue to find that pattern over and over again, no matter how painful the pattern is.

I was raised with a specific view of what life is "assumed" to be. The plan was simple. Graduate high school, go to college, meet a man, get a good nine-to-five , get married, have children. However, it was very obvious that this was not the path I was on. I tried to convince myself that it would all just magically fall into place, but truthfully I was lost. I didn't know how to get back on track. I felt isolated from the world around me. I was in denial and couldn't seem to figure out how to change the course of my existence so instead I continued to escape reality.

Let's dive a little deeper.

My parents divorced when I was 11, and there is trauma behind that experience that opened wounds of abandonment, safety, and insecurity that buried themselves deep within my being. With a lot of healing work, I have been able to come to the conclusion that everyone did the best they could with what they knew or believed to be good, but even the best intentions can cause harm. For me, although my childhood was filled with everything I could possibly need, it was missing a sense of familial intimacy that is necessary for emotional and social development.

From the ages of 15 to 26, I was riding a downward spiral that turned into a complete trainwreck. It began with what I thought was a typical teenage rebellious phase.

At 17, I suffered a tremendous loss that was both devastating and traumatizing. My first love was lost to a drinking and driving accident. I will never forget the emotions that were conjured from this incident. The most significant being the feeling of abandonment.

Grief is a strange phenomena. Everyone deals with death differently. But at this young age, I was not yet accustomed to this type of mature thinking. I found out the hard way that during times of death, people need someone to blame and overnight I became the easy target. I was not only left behind by my boyfriend (figuratively of course), I was eventually shunned by his family and friends. I felt completely alone, with no one to turn to.

I tumbled further down the rabbit hole than I already was. I fell into a space of depression and anxiety that my teenage brain could not cope with. I felt that I needed to hide my feelings, which turned into a common theme for me.

This was just one of the many catalysts to the life's journey I was on. There was a consistent pattern of behaviors and choices that kept recurring within my story. In college, I found myself in a toxic relationship that was physically, mentally and emotionally abusive. Soon thereafter, I was in my early twenties and a complete hot mess. I managed to graduate but could not hold a job, didn't have any real connection with anyone, and could not manage or regulate my own actions, behaviors, or emotions.

Continuous repetitive behaviors eventually became worse and worse. I was beaten emotionally and spiritually, finding myself at rock bottom. I was 26 with no aspirations, no career goals, no ability to make decisions for myself, no relationships, and was exiled from almost my entire family. I felt hopeless, useless, and destined for failure. Something needed to change, or else I was going to continue onto the bitter end of my life, living within a miserable existence. The pain was great enough. It was time to change. It was time for me to put in the work to create a life worth living.

Chapter 2: The Beginning

Affirmation

I am safe to be courageous.

I am safe to walk through fears.

I am safe to move through changes.

*I am safe to transform
into the strongest version of myself.*

Transform (verb)

trans·form

    a: to change in composition or structure

    b: to change the outward form or appearance of

    c: to change in character or condition : convert

Most transformation processes begin with a major change. For me, this change was solely based on lifestyle choices. In September of 2016, I made a conscious decision to reconstruct my life. I made a commitment to myself that I was going to do whatever it took to create a life worth living. At the time, I wasn't exactly sure what that meant, but that is part of the process.

I joined a program of recovery that promotes growth through community and self-reflection. The practices I adopted here pushed me to establish a vulnerable connection to my feelings, and brought upon a level of healing that changed the game for me. I began to embrace spiritual principles such as honesty, open-mindedness, and willingness. I started to let go of ego and self-pity so I could take ownership for my past actions, and responsibility for my future.

Affirmations are in essence positive self-talk, used to attract the energy you seek to create in your life. The amazing part of my story is that I was harnessing this energetic practice before I even realized it.

In early recovery, I had the mindset of "I can and I will." Using this new found confidence and belief in myself, with only three months clean, I found a job, reinstated my drivers license, bought a car, and began renting my very first apartment. All of these things seemed to just fall into my lap. I kept doing the next right thing. I maintained positive thinking. And when I wanted something, I *knew* I could have it. I had a mentality of willingness, commitment, focus, and faith. All things that will be addressed within the teachings in this book.

In 2018, I became a certified yoga instructor. I began to expand my connections with others as I became a part of a beautiful yoga community. I learned about yogic philosophies and Buddhist traditions that opened my mind to new spiritual practices .

The support I was receiving from like-minded people was so valuable in my process of self-discovery. Along the way I have been so blessed to have met many different people on their own healing paths, each sharing their experiences and enabling my own growth.

Physical movement became a solid foundation in my routine. This awakened a deep passion for health and wellness. In 2019, I enrolled in a Master's program for Health and Physical Education. I fell in love with expanding my knowledge, which fed my desire to learn.

I was *doing* a lot of *things*. Recovery, exercise, meditation, reading, school, teaching. But something was missing. My mind and body were being taken care of outwardly, but I still had the tendency to get fixated on my feelings. This fixation would become obsessive, which would often become toxic. I needed to try something new to help me face my feelings and begin to focus on the positive.

In 2021, I constructed my own self-affirmation practice. For years, I had heard of affirmations but never truly explored it myself. There are many books, countless scientific studies, and major public figures like Oprah Winfey and comedian Jim Carey, who back its effectiveness.

I knew I needed to shift my mindset from negative to positive. I wanted to elevate my ability to focus on exactly what I wanted in life and begin to create it, one intentional goal at a time.

The practice is all about connecting to who you are. It is creating self-validation to help you achieve your dreams and desires. I continuously use the practice of affirmations to create the best version of myself. I have attracted opportunities and experiences. I have manifested an abundant career. I found freedom within myself. All the things I've called into existence at one point seemed unattainable, but I continued to shift the narrative, connect to my words, and stayed in the work.

The book you are holding in your hands right now is enough proof of this practice manifesting into my life. This is an actual product of the affirmations that are explained within these pages.

As I began to put my life back together, lost dreams awakened within me that were suppressed by dark and gloom for so long. As a teenager, I would envision myself having a career as a writer. I've always kept journals, taken classes on journalism and creative writing, played around with freelance publication, and at one point even had a blog.

I'll admit I was 100% influenced by Sara Jessica Parker's depiction of Carrie Bradshaw in the 90's TV series, Sex and the City. I loved the character's writing style and how she addressed real life scenarios that people could learn from or relate to. I have always been able to express myself through writing better than any other form of communication. It was a secret desire of mine to compose a book, and in my journey of self-discovery, I was able to tap into that calling, now qualified to dub myself an author.

The use of affirmations in the process of creating this book not only developed the actual content, but also kept me grounded and centered within my confidence. Without the relationship I have cultivated with myself, this book would not exist. I would have drowned in self-doubt before completion.

More evidence of the effectiveness of this practice can be found in how I used affirmations to attract a career that gave me purpose. After going back to school at the age of 29, I was met with an overwhelming amount of fear and doubt that was being projected onto me by other people. I decided to ignore the chatter and stay the course.

I was finally on the verge of graduation, when new fears started to creep in. There I was, almost 31 and just beginning the job search as an educator. I had gone all in on this goal. I had to find a way to quiet the noise and remember that, "I can and I will."

I focused my affirmation practice specifically on career goals and abundance. On the verge of graduation, I began writing affirmations stating - "I will have a full time teaching position," and by January I landed my first job.

My life was coming together, at an undeniable speed that kept me hopeful, focused, and self-assured. The best, and the worst, were yet to come.

There are times on this journey where I felt "I have arrived," and times where I have been humbled by the unexpected trials. Whether I was using affirmations to attract the things I wanted, or using them to pick myself up after I've fallen, this practice has been, and will continue to be, ongoing. Even on the not so great days, I can find joy because of the practices that are written in this book.

Chapter 3: The Now

Affirmation

I let go of expectations,
& allow myself to feel the energy of peace.

I welcome new possibilities,
& explore opportunities to
practice growth.

I appreciate the process of healing,
& embrace the experiences of my journey.

All is manifesting for me NOW.

Practice (verb)

prac·tice

> **a:** carry out, apply.
> **b:** to do or perform often, customarily, or habitually.

There have been many lessons that I had to endure throughout this process that have each exposed great realizations that have helped me adopt a new way of living. Each experience, each lesson, has helped me crawl out of the dark and into a world filled with light and opportunity.

Process and practice are important tools when coming face to face with life lessons. Your life is a series of processes. Simple actions that lead to specific results. Every choice you make, leads to different outcomes. When choosing to embrace your own power, it takes time, and continued practice is necessary.

How did I get to where I am now?

Step one, accept the truth that no one is coming to save you.

After years of waiting to be rescued, I eventually figured out that I had to put in the work to save myself. The thing about healing is, the work needs to come from within and it's never really *complete*. There is no endpoint or final arrival. The practice of affirmations, for me, is a tool that I continuously use to manifest the things that I want to attract into my life. and believe me those wants and needs will change and evolve as you continue on your own journey.

Step two, understand that you are not, and cannot, be perfect.

To be human is to be perfectly imperfect. Accepting this, is how you continue to grow and move forward on your path. As you strive to become better, you will continue to put in work, build your resilience, and connect to your own uniqueness. You are individual to yourself. There may be people who are similar and like minded, but there is no one else in this lifetime that is exactly you.

Honor that!

Your personal energy is a connection to yourself. Acceptance of your imperfections and seeing them as assets within your life, is a magical way of coming to love yourself for who you are in each and every moment.

Step three, love yourself.

In order to connect to the frequency of self-love, you must reroute your thinking from negative to positive, which can easily be achieved with commitment to your own practice.

I follow my affirmation practice as a daily routine. I write a weekly affirmation, worded in the present tense, every Sunday morning. I read it out loud every single day, as if it already exists, to solidify the intention and speak the vibration into the universe.

There is great value in becoming comfortable with speaking affirmations out loud. To speak out loud is to voice your personal vibration into reality by sending that energy into the universe from your own lips.

As you continue on this journey, you will learn about vibration, frequency and energy, and how the intersection of all three helps connect you to your desired goals. Energy exists all around you and within you. It is a vibration. It is frequency. The goal of affirmations is to match your vibrational frequency, a.k.a. your energy, with the vibrational frequency of the universe, to mirror the energy of your intentions. *This concept is repeatedly integrated throughout this process.*

How do you do this? You align your vibration with peace and calmness.

If we cultivate peace within ourselves,
then clarity, compassion, and courage will arise.
"How to See," by Thich Nhat Hanh

Peace is not cultivated with *things*. Peace is cultivated from within. A connection to core principles, such as acceptance, will help you connect with your own internal happiness, instead of seeking outside *things* for validation. It is in this state of inner peace and fulfillment that you can manifest the life you truly desire. Why?

Manifesting inner peace and happiness is manifesting personal power. This is the source of your creation energy!

True inner peace comes from **Step four. Trust yourself.**

Trusting myself and my own intuitive guidance has brought me to where I am today. I had to become willing to take risks in order to get where I wanted to be, but also embrace a connection to inner peace by trusting the universe and letting go of attachment to specific outcomes.

Six months after beginning my first job, I received an offer at a public school that was much closer to my home. The only caveat being, it wasn't a long term position. Tapping into the space of trust, I decided to walk through fear and take the job because it was more aligned for me, even though there was zero job security.

During this time, I was coincidentally experiencing significant changes that created instability in my personal life. I found solace in my affirmation practice, which kept me open to new possibilities and focused on creating safety from within myself.

The peaceful connection I was creating was met with a gift from the universe. Not long after I took the leap and accepted the position, I was awarded a secure position at a district that I never would've thought would be the perfect fit, but magically, it was.

Practicing self-affirmations elevated my process as I began to attract the vibration of safety and security. Letting go of expectations was the start of cultivating my own validation and creating a solid foundation of spiritual trust. This took practice. It did not come overnight.

I'd be lying if I didn't admit to times of energetic blockages in my ability to attract positivity. I've experienced loss, divorce, and periods of extreme self-doubt along the way. I openly share my stories, the good and the bad, to reveal that even when life decides to "show up," you have the ability to continue the work, as long as you keep a positive mindset. This is a process and like most there will be great jumps forward, paired with a few setbacks along the way.

You are now beginning a journey of self-healing. This is the moment where you can decide to take control of your life. As you continue, I offer the suggestion to begin the exercise of writing. The journal prompts within this book will help you decipher your thoughts and experiences. Remember, processes are not linear. Sometimes it's a zig zag, and sometimes you are going in circles. Just embrace the adventure. Don't over think. Just close your eyes, connect to your breath, and begin to write.

Chapter 4: The Magic of Affirmations

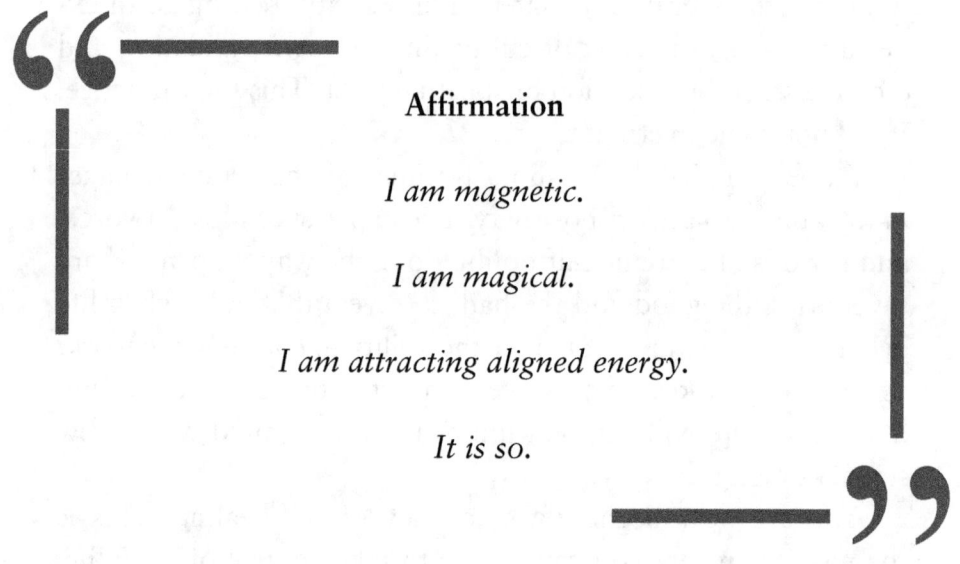

Affirmation

I am magnetic.

I am magical.

I am attracting aligned energy.

It is so.

Attract (verb)

at·tract

: to pull to or draw toward oneself or itself

What are affirmations?

When thinking of the word *affirmation*, my first thought always goes to the term "affirm." By definition the word affirm is to state as a fact, or to assertively or confidently say something. In this context, affirmations are statements that you are speaking into existence, or words that you are using to manifest your reality.

In layman's terms, affirmations are positive words that help to change a person's mindset or thought process. But in magical terms, affirmations are powerful words that help people create the lives they intend to live.

The purpose of this practice is to attract positive energy into your life. You attract the energy that you speak. If you are focused on negative things, negative energy is attracted to you and therefore negative things often happen. The universe responds to the frequency you are projecting. This is why the language you use is sacred.

Speaking daily affirmations is an exercise of retraining your brain. It shifts perspectives and rewires old thought patterns. The mind is very powerful and it will pick up patterns in order to "protect" itself. This means the brain will always follow the path of least resistance, defaulting to the thought pattern that it is *used* to. Affirmations help to reroute thoughts, like negative thinking or complaining, and allows you to view things in a different light.

Now, if you aren't a full believer in the magic of affirmations just yet, or you are on the fence, let's dive into the actual science behind the theories of positive self-talk. Science is alchemy and alchemy is magic, therefore science is magic. It's all interconnected.

Studies have shown that affirmations increase confidence and self-worth, but the real magic is how positive self-talk can change your actual thinking. The brain creates patterns based on your memories, which is called a *schema*. Basically, your brain will lump together any and all experiences that are similar to one specific experience and use that experience to anticipate a possible conclusion. As you continue to have experiences in your life, you continue to develop schemas. Eventually the brain develops patterns it is comfortable with, often leading people to repeat the same behaviors, even when it is clear that it is not good for them.

Daily affirmations can train your brain into new patterns that will become automatic over time. This is not to say that your original way of thinking will completely diminish from your mind, but you will be able to identify the pattern, and change your reactions before you fall into the old way of doing things.

It's important to be aware of the fact that you can self-prophesize your own outcomes with the words you choose to use. If you feel a sense of "threat" by a thought, then you are already setting yourself up for failure. *Threats* can be judgment of others, stereotypes, being overwhelmed, self-doubt, distrust, fear, etc. If any threat changes your thought process into believing you cannot do something, because of a belief or judgment, that becomes dangerous for the manifester.

Dr. Claude M. Steele, social psychologist and professor, revealed that these perceived *threats* can affect your self-identity. Shifting the mindset back to a positive intention and using affirmations for self-assurance will help lead the brain back to a state of positive thought patterns. Ultimately, this mindset reset realigns you with your sense of self, your core beliefs, and values.

So, how do you stay away from threatening, a.k.a negative, thoughts? Knowing yourself and your core values. This will help you stay focused on the things that you truly want. Sifting through the BS of what others think and really connecting to your dreams is how you can take this practice from basic to magic. Forget about the "supposed to," or "have to," lies you tell yourself based on familial beliefs or things you learned as a kid. Really sit with yourself and think about what drives you, what is important to you. Knowing your core values will in turn attract those things into your own life, on your own terms.

As you think you vibrate.
As you vibrate you attract.
- Abraham Hicks

In my own personal practice, I utilize affirmations to attract positive experiences into my life based on the things I value. I created a morning ritual, which is just a witchy term for routine, to help me stay focused on my intentions. I wake up each day, read my weekly affirmation, make a gratitude list, and meditate on what it is I am calling (a.k.a. attracting) into my life.

The honest truth is that I can be a complainer. When I began my road to recovery, this character flaw was brought to my attention real quick. I never noticed it before and the identification made me painfully aware of it. This pain prompted change. Early on in my affirmation practice, my intentions were simply to stay grateful and vibrate positive energy.

I clearly remember when the words began to affect my mindset and eventually affected my actual life. I was sitting in a classroom, at the end of my first semester in a physical education master's program. The holidays were approaching and it was my 30th birthday so I began to reflect on what exactly I wanted for my future. At this point I had just over three years in recovery and was living my life according to spiritual principles that were aligning me to my life's purpose.

I knew at that moment, sitting in a room filled with peers that were almost all six years younger than me, that I had a goal and a purpose that was much greater than I could even imagine. I had already taught yoga for about two years at this point and I knew teaching overall health and wellness was my true calling.

I started to see that my purpose was pulling me in a different direction, away from physical education. I wanted my students to know *the what, the why, and the how*. To me, this is how I could contribute to healing the next generation and I knew that I wouldn't be able to do it in the gym.

I clearly recall turning to a classmate at that moment and stating, "I'm going to teach health."

The response was what I expected, "Yes, getting your health certification will make you more marketable as a physical education teacher."

"No, I mean I only want to teach health."

"Do they even have *just* health teachers? Usually it's split now with PE teachers."

"That's true, but I'm going to be a health teacher."

I remember stating this firmly, with zero doubt in my mind that it would be true. I'm not exactly sure what came over me. I just knew it at that moment. It was a fact.

I could see the doubt in my classmate's eyes. It wasn't the first time I saw that look within that same year. Months prior, I got that same look from my father when I told him I wanted to go back to school to get a degree in education. His fears were seeping out of his pores being completely projected onto me, "It'll be really hard to find a job. Isn't 30 a little old to become a teacher?"

My reaction was the same, "I will find a job," which turned into an ongoing mantra during my entire three years of schooling.

And I did land a job immediately after earning my degree. It was PE but I still knew where I would end up. A year and a half after starting my teaching career, I began a full-time health position.

Affirmation
I am attracting a positive energy.
I am attracting a higher vibration.
I am attracting a confident frequency.

Attraction is the key concept here. To attract is to draw something towards you. Using words to attract the energy you want to receive is how you tap into your vibrational energy, aligning it with universal energy, and bringing all potential outcomes into your life.

It is all about the vibration that you are putting into the world. To fine tune your vibration, is to attract the exact energy you want. At this time in my life, I was focused on projecting positive energy outward, in turn calling back to me exactly what I wanted, and then was able to receive it. Magical isn't it?

I've been known to call my practice "affirmation spells" because it's all about creating a poetic sequence of words that are individual to the person who is creating it. In the Universe there are millions of potential outcomes that exist. Anything is possible. Tuning into that belief, you allow those possibilities into your existence, and align yourself with your internal magic.

Journal prompts:

1. *Create a list of core values that you feel a deep connection with.*
2. *Create your own affirmation to help you release negative thinking to focus on positive energy. (you can use your core values to create this)*

Example: I release any and all negative thoughts. I think positively to align with _____.

Chapter 5: I Am

Affirmation

I am confident.
I manifest & create my reality.

I am successful.
I have endless potential & possibilities in my life.

I am worthy.
I deserve all of my dreams & intentions.

I am. I am. I am.

Confidence (noun)

con·fi·dence

: a feeling or consciousness of one's powers or of reliance on one's circumstances

Here is a fact; positive self-talk increases your confidence. Yes, I said FACT. A 2022 study found that athletes use this practice to enhance their success. When positive self-talk was measured with negative self-talk, the ones who could affirm themselves with uplifting words, always performed better. This is because they had more self-confidence. Even famous athletes like Kobe Bryant and Michael Jordan have used this theory to excel in their careers by boosting their confidence and therefore their performance.

The practice of affirming yourself is the practice of realizing your own personal power. The perfect way to begin to connect to this power is by constructing "I am" statements to increase your self-confidence.

There is a common misconception that you need other people to *fix* you, whether that be a doctor, mentor, teacher, or a holistic practitioner. In truth, you are your own healer. You have the ability to heal yourselves with your own vibration, whether the vibration is positive thinking or spoken words. This is your power. It resides within each and every one of us. All you need to do is to believe you are significant and worthy, and align that belief with your words using self-affirmations. This increases your integrity and confidence by matching your words and actions with your values and beliefs.

Don't get me wrong, I still love being validated by others. However, I now know and truly believe that I don't *need* outside praise. The power to validate yourself comes from within. As you connect to your confidence, by affirming your own self-worth, you are becoming the creator of your own reality.

Stop acting so small.
You are the universe in ecstatic motion.
– Rumi

While writing the pages of this book, I was suddenly struck with an overwhelming sense of fear, self-doubt and imposter syndrome.

Imposter syndrome is an invasive feeling of self-doubt regarding your own skills, abilities, or knowledge. It makes you feel like a fraud, or *imposter*, doubting your own intelligence and making you feel less than.

These feelings are no stranger to me, as I have been dealing with them ever since I was a little girl. The way I used to process these feelings was through validation from others, but in this case I was actually triggered by the lack of validation I was getting. Call it irony, call it coincidence, but I call it yet another opportunity to experience a lesson that I still continue to learn.

After I "finished" chapter one of this book, I was hit with a huge wave of insecurity. I submitted the draft to my publisher for feedback and was expecting all positive words about how great I am. The feedback wasn't necessarily bad, but it wasn't exactly what I was seeking. She asked me to change the sequence of the chapter which sounded easy enough but when I actually sat down to do it, I experienced such resistance. I got frustrated.

I became defiant. I immediately reached out to my support group of authors to get a hit of outside validation, seeking to fuel my need for instant gratification and help regulate my nervous system.

The problem here? I was in the middle of writing a book all about teaching others to affirm themselves but wasn't using my own practices in the process. This right here was the universe gifting me an experience to help me see where there's still work to be done.

As I was sending a voice recording to a fellow writer, venting about how I wasn't good enough, I heard myself and stopped. *Words are powerful.* As I was speaking, I was processing, and in the process I came to the realization of the lesson at hand. I began to ask myself; *Why am I writing this book? Why am I going through this process with a support group of authors and publishers, if I wasn't going to be able to take constructive criticism and be open to feedback?*

I share this experience to express that I am human and I am not perfect. Even with this daily practice I still have days where I struggle. You too will have days filled with frustration and what feels like regression, but it's not. It's all about practice, not perfection. The more awareness you have around the times that you may be falling short, is growth in itself.

The key is to see the patterned thinking, identify it, accept it, and then change the behavior. Eventually the old ways of thinking will become less engrained. Awareness is part of your power. When you are aware of your patterns, you then have the ability to change them.

My practice began with "I am," statements. This simple but powerful method helped me create a new way of thinking. I started by focusing on three (or more) things that I wanted to cultivate into my life and created a sentence for each starting with "I am."

Affirmation

I am grateful. I am stable. I am courageous.
I am. I am. I am.

Using "I am" affirmations is just the first step to help you connect to your personal power. The real magic lies within the ability to embrace your power, align the brain and the heart, and create the vision you seek. As you continue on this path of developing your own affirmation language, you will begin to evolve your style of speech. Using words that connect to specific meanings will elevate your affirmation practice.

The chart below contains "I" statements that connect to specific meanings. Using this system will enhance your practice and allow you to manifest on a deeper, more intentional level.

"I" Statement	Meaning
"I am"	Safety, groundedness, survival
"I Feel"	Creation, passion, desires
"I Attract"	Confidence, security, intellect
"I Love"	Love, compassion, trust
"I Speak"	Communication, voice, acceptance
"I See"	Focus, perception,
"I Understand"	Connection, freedom

As you grow on this journey, remember it all begins with "I am," which is the source of safety and groundedness. Feeling safe, feeling capable, and feeling confident to go for your goals comes from being connected to self and being grounded within your world.

Confidence equals security within your own being. This is not a suggestion of cockiness but a suggestion of knowing who you are, while being humble enough to understand that you are here on this earth to continue learning. Finding the balance of humility and confidence will help you continue to connect to your personal power, as well as, the power of the universe.

Like all other things, without a secure foundation you will be blocked by unsteady energy. Build your base strong with affirmations of confidence, safety and security. From there, all possibilities will arise and your dreams will awaken in the process.

Journal prompt:

1. *What makes you feel safe?*
2. *What drives your passion and creativity?*
3. *What makes you feel love/loved?*
4. *What sparks your voice?*
5. *What keeps you focused?*
6. *What helps you feel connected?*
7. *Using the examples from the chapter, create an affirmation using "I am..."*

Chapter 6: Words Are Power

"

Affirmation

I am in tune with my language,
my personal vibration & source of connection.

I am aligned with self-expression,
tapping into confidence & positive vibration.

My words are my power &
my sovereignty,
the link to higher energetic frequency.

It is innately mine.

"

Language (noun)

lan·guage

 a: the words, their pronunciation, and the methods of combining them used and understood by a community.

 b: a systematic means of communicating ideas or feelings by the use of conventionalized signs, sounds, gestures, or marks having understood meanings

Words, or language of any kind, are a deep expression of emotions that is individual to humankind, on this planet at least. Language is used to communicate, to tell stories, to connect with others, to connect with feelings, and to connect with yourself.

Remember, the voice is a vibration and this vibration is uniquely, powerfully, your own. Your words are an energetic exchange with the universe, and the universe will match the frequency that you are projecting outwards. The trick to creating the reality that you desire is to focus on holding the energetic vibration. Hold the feeling and vision, and it will eventually be matched, and then created.

My artistic and emotional expression has always come from the use of words, whether it was writing or speaking. Words are beautiful. Words have power. Words can manifest into reality.

I believe in making daily life magical in some way or another. I do this by connecting to nature, movement, rituals, and poetic affirmations that use specific language making it feel like some sort of magical *spell*.

The use of words to call in specific outcomes is not a new concept. For thousands of years, humans have been connecting the frequency of words to better their lives with the use of prayer, mantra, intention setting, and spells.

The first known prayer dates back to 200 A.D., which means human beings have been using words to voice their desires for over 1,800 years. In my humble opinion, there isn't much difference between the concept of prayer and spells. Both prayers and spells use language to send out energy. Both are the practice of aligning words to a positive vibration. Both are used to attract positive energy in your life, and both are wholeheartedly believed to come true because of faith. Therefore prayer, affirmations, and spells are really all the same. It doesn't matter what you call it.

The idea is to connect to your words and align with something, anything, that you believe in. This connection will guide you through the process of your journey. If you don't know exactly what your belief is, start with connection to a power greater than yourself, a high power if you will. This is universal source, whether you call it God or not. Tapping into this energy will help you connect to the energy you seek.

God has no religion.
- Mahatma Gandhi

When I began my journey of recovery I didn't have a concept of faith that I lived by. I was brought up with Christian values; baptized, received communion and confirmation, but I never really had a deep belief in organized religion. Going to church just felt forced or fake. As an adult, I can see now that my adverse feelings to religion stemmed from the fact that I was "just doing what I was told to do." I didn't really understand why church was important only on Sundays or holidays, and the actions of those around me didn't necessarily match the scriptures of religious beliefs.

My journey to healing needed faith and trust. I began to develop my own system of belief that has grown, and continues to grow, since beginning on the path of self-resurrection.

I am very grateful for the life experiences I've had in this process because I have taken pieces from each, developing an eclectic form of spiritual practice that is fine tuned and makes sense for me. This is a hidden gem that most people don't know. You can create your own belief system. You can create your own spiritual practices. You can develop a belief in your own higher power that works for you and only you.

In 2022, I attended a retreat in Costa Rica that enhanced my relationship with language. I learned how to sequence my words to call upon energies that I wanted to align with, as well as ancient practices to raise my vibration and connect to universal source.

I remember being in awe with the powerful women who were attending this magical retreat, most of which had very esoteric backgrounds. This experiential trip expanded my knowledge on so many levels. I learned new terminology, such as "it is so," the structure of calling in elements, and the wording of wiccan inspired *spells*. I learned how to blend movement, energy, and words into one practice which deepened my connection to my higher power, my voice, and myself.

I began to incorporate this new knowledge into my spiritual practices, specifically using the statement, "It is so" or "so it is." These words are solidifying that the things you are speaking already exist. It is an expression of confirmation, stating a fact that just IS.

Affirmation

I am present in this moment.
I am grateful for the experience of now.
I am at peace with all that is.
It is so.

As you connect to the value of your words, you will begin to examine and understand the influence your language has on what you are attracting. Your words, thoughts and actions all play a role in what is being brought into your life. If you can maintain an intentional focus on positive things, words, and experiences, you can then attract more of the same.

You have the power to choose your words. Being intentional is how the magic happens. Without clear intentions, your focus is blurry. Without belief in your intention, your alignment is unsteady. The word intention is all about having a purpose. When you put intention behind your words, you are clear on what exactly it is you are asking for, working towards, or aligning with.

The power behind your language is your intention. This is all a part of your vibrational energy, which you are projecting outwardly into the universe. In order to attract what you desire, you first need to adopt the principles of honesty, awareness, acceptance, and openness. It is with the practice of these specific principles that you can connect to who you are, what you want, and how you will get it.

Journal prompts:

1. *What is your connection to words, language and speaking?*
2. *Is it easy for you to use words to express yourself?*
3. *Do you feel your words are powerful? If not, identify the blockages that keep you from expressing your words.*
4. *Create an affirmation using an I am statement, paired with a specific intention.*

Example: I am abundant. I am focused on achieving financial stability.

Section Two
"I Feel."

You're Personal Power,
(You Are Personal Power).

"

Affirmation

*I feel into the essence of who I am,
fully secure within myself.*

*I feel into the space of hope & faith,
self-assured within the
present moment.*

*I feel into the power that resides within my being,
trusting that all is being manifested.*

It is so.

"

Self-assurance (noun)

:great faith in oneself or one's abilities : as in confidence

Personal power is a very distinct unique entity that lives inside each and every person. It is the ability to change and adapt. The ability to create and manifest. Your connection to your personal power begins with your connection to self.

Within the next section, I invite you to be reintroduced to self by adopting specific principles that will allow you to see who you are, to understand how you work, and to trust the process of your growth. It's within the commitment to practicing honesty, awareness, and acceptance that ignites the expansion of your thoughts into new ways of thinking and behaving.

It starts with one simple, but complex, concept; honesty. When you can take an honest look at who you are, you can then find alignment in what you want to call into your life by examining how you are currently living, and seeing if it matches up to the energy you want to receive.

Once you are aware of yourself and see who you truly are, you have the ability to find acceptance for self and open your mind to where you may need to make changes in order to step fully into the center of your power.

This is the beginning of the journey to discovering who you are and what you are capable of. This is the ability to fully step into self-assurance, confidence, and action.

It begins now.

Chapter 7: Breathe, Rest, Repeat.

Affirmation

Tuning into the body.
I am rooted & secure.

Tuning into the mind.
I am peaceful & clear.

Tuning into the heart.
I am light & love.

Tuning into the breath.
I am alive & free.

Emotion (noun)
emo·tion

a: a conscious mental reaction (such as anger or fear) subjectively experienced as strong feeling usually directed toward a specific object and typically accompanied by physiological and behavioral changes in the body

b: a state of feeling

Emotions can be very real roadblocks, but emotions do not own you. Your feelings are real and valid, but they are also fleeting and fluid, changing each moment. You do not need to let your emotions over run your life, and this is where self-regulation comes into play.

In this process, you will obtain the awareness to identify emotions and triggers, pinpointing what causes you to feel the way you do. There are tools you can use to help regulate your nervous system, calm the body and mind, and be in a state of homeostasis. This is the mind-body connection.

The connection is through the nervous system which is composed of the *central nervous system*, which is the brain and spinal cord, and the *peripheral nervous system,* which are the nerves that branch out from the spine.

The peripheral nervous system is made up of two parts, the somatic nervous system, voluntary movements in the physical body, and the autonomic nervous system, involuntary movements and reactions.

The autonomic nervous system controls emotional reactions and consists of the *parasympathetic and sympathetic systems.*

These are automatic responses to experiences that are being had in the brain.

The parasympathetic nervous system is known as "rest and digest," and is the state you are in when you feel regulated and relaxed. This is the ideal place for your body to be in because it is centered, balanced, and calm. The effects of the outside world makes it impossible to be in this regulated state 24/7. With self-awareness, you have the ability to understand and use specific coping mechanisms that can bring you back to this state, if and when you become dysregulated.

The sympathetic nervous system is known as "fight or flight." This is the state you're in when you are dysregulated and reacting to something that is making you feel unsafe or uneasy. You will be in this state when you are stressed, anxious, overwhelmed, overstimulated, or fearful. This occurs a lot throughout the day. It may sound a little dramatic, but think about the amount of stress that you may experience on a day to day basis There are a range of things that can trigger uninvited thoughts based on fear, self-doubt, failure, and underperforming.

Modern society does not stimulate the parasympathetic nervous system. It actually constantly puts people into a state of fight or flight. This is why self-regulation is important. You cannot completely avoid stress because it is a part of the current world, but you can find ways to help you stay centered when your emotions get the best of you.

Why am I doing a mini lesson on the nervous system in a book about affirmations?

Simple.

Self-regulation is crucial when manifesting dreams and desires because in a calm state, you can clearly see your goal, and know how to achieve it in the best way possible. If you are not regulated, you are not in tune with the energetic vibrations of the universe because your energy will be tense and uneasy.

Understanding the nervous system and how your thoughts affect your physical body will help you understand how to become regulated and stay the course during emotional dysregulation, which will occur on your manifestation journey.

Self-affirmations are an amazing tool to help with emotional regulation. The use of positive words activates positive thinking in the mind, allowing the body to relax into a state of rest and digest.

Breathe.

Breathing in, I calm body and mind.
Breathing out, I smile.
Dwelling in the present moment,
I know this is the only moment.
- Thich Nhat Hanh

Breathing is one of the most significant tools to use for regulation.

Your breath is your *prana*, meaning "life-giving" force. Without breath, you would cease to exist on this timeline. Being able to tap into this life giving power is the ability to control the body and mind. It is such a power to claim when you have the ability to control your breathing. This enhances your ability to remain centered and grounded, and it also brings about a deeper awareness of self.

Some breathing practices are simple and can be easily accessed any time, any where, like box breathing and retention breath. Others can be a little more complex, such as Wim Hoff breathing and Holotropic breathwork. Using a simple breathing technique, paired with affirmations, can increase your connection to your manifestations in an impactful way. Bringing the mind and body together is the act of tapping into your personal power through easeful, calm energy.

Journal Prompt:

1. *Pick a breathing technique from the chart. Commit to practicing the technique 3-4 times a week, for about 3-5 minutes a session. Journal any feelings that arise during your practice.*
2. *Use the following affirmation while breathing;*

As you breathe in think "breathing in," and as you breathe out, think "breathing out." (From the practice of Thich Nhat Hanh)

Chapter 7: Breath, Rest, Repeat.

Name of Practice	How to do it
Box Breathing *Breath in for a count of 4* *Hold your breath for a count of 4* *Breath out for a count of 4* *Hold on empty lunges for a count of 4* *Repeat for 1-3 minutes (add time as you become more accumulated to the practice)*	Box breathing is a technique that involves equal length inhalation and exhalation. The most common practice is a 4:4:4:4 ratio of breathing and retention breath, however it can be any number of equal counts. Starting with 4 is ideal and once it becomes easy you can increase to 5,6,7, or even 8. **Benefits:** lowers stress, calms the mind, activates parasympathetic nervous system, improves focus and clarity.
3 Part Breath *Find a comfortable position, lying down.* *Inhale to a third of your lungs' capacity then pause for 2-3 seconds.* *Inhale another third and pause, and then repeat once more and pause.* *Option for full exhale before going to the second round, or exhaling in the same pattern as the inhale.* *Repeat for 5 rounds.*	This breathing practice involves pausing your inhalations and/or exhalations with brief holds. With each pause, you are filling the lunges slightly more and more each time. It is good to practice first with the inhalation, using no holds as you exhale and build your way up over time. This practice brings awareness not only to the breath but also to the lungs/the body. **Benefits:** calms the mind, releases tension, lowers heart rate, and promotes relaxation.
Alternate Nostril Breath *Using the right hand, bring your middle finger and pointer finger together, bend the ring and pinky fingers down. Using the thumb and ring/pinky finger to close off the nostrils (alternating)* *Gently close your right nostril with your right thumb. Inhale through your left nostril, then close it with your ring finger and pinky. After a very brief pause, open and exhale slowly through the right nostril. Keep the right nostril open, inhale, then close it, and open and exhale slowly through the left. This is one cycle.* *Repeat 3 to 5 times, then release the hand mudra and go back to normal breathing.*	This breath is known as a channel cleansing breath to help align the Nadis which are energy channels in the body. This breath clears the breathing pathways and cleanses the energy channels to bring about a mind-body connection. **Benefits:** eases stress and anxiety, enhances relaxation, balances the mind, and lowers heart rate

Rest.

Meditation is an amazing asset. It quiets the mind and allows you to completely surrender to the present moment. It is a practice of contemplation and reflection where you can take time to focus on the present moment. It's within the moment of now where you can hear and see your heart's desires most clearly.

I want to begin by expressing that meditation takes practice. It's a mental exercise. I often hear people saying that they "can't meditate," and my response is always the same. It takes time, patience and consistency. If you think of the brain as a muscle, you can agree that it takes time to build strength. You cannot randomly walk into a gym and expect to deadlift 300 lbs if you've never done so before. This concept applies to your brain as well.

In order to train your brain to become accustomed to meditation, I suggest starting small and building your way up. Begin with an amount of time that is achievable for you, maybe five minutes, maybe two. Make it consistent by doing the practice every day for four to six weeks. Build the habit slowly, with patience for yourself, and then begin to increase the time, remembering to make your intended progress attainable. It's also a good idea to meditate at the same time each day, usually either first thing in the morning or just before bed. Keeping a journal can be helpful during this process to see how you are evolving over time.

There are many resources for meditation, and also different types. You can explore silent meditation, the use of calming music, or try guided meditations. There are apps, such as Calm and Headspace. There are programs you can follow led by major names like Dr. Joe Dispanza and Tony Robbins. And there are tons of free resources too. Youtube is my personal favorite. Here you can find a wide variety of meditations by simply searching for something like *five minute meditation*. You can also get more specific and search meditations for abundance, joy, even manifestation.

Trying different styles of meditations is a good exercise until you find something you truly connect with. This can be the content, the music, or a person's voice. It doesn't really matter exactly what you're drawn to, as long as you find some type of connection to enable consistency in your practice.

> *The whole world opens when we accept*
> *this moment,*
> *this very moment.*
> – Deepak Chopra

My meditation story begins in the Winter of 2020. My main source of meditation in those earlier years were moving meditations, such as working out, running, or yoga. These coping mechanisms were helpful but I started to see that I needed more help to increase my focus, strengthen my mind, and maintain a sense of peace and calmness.

The catalyst to this new found motivation to begin a more traditional practice of mediation began when I was invited to participate in a meditation group on Facebook. It was a 21-day abundance challenge, using journal prompts and meditation recordings by Deepak Chopra, an American-Indian author, also referred to as a *new age guru*.

I committed myself to the full three weeks and took it very seriously. I answered every journal prompt and didn't miss one day of the meditations. I saw a significant change in my behaviors, my stress levels, and my general outlook on life. So of course, the addict in me wanted more.

I then began to explore the work of Dr. Joe Dispenza, another big time name in meditation practices and self-healing techniques. I found a lot of recordings that focused on brain and heart coherence. I really felt connected to this idea because of my overwhelming, overthinking, mentality and constant struggle to connect to my heart. I would listen to the same meditation for one to two weeks before switching it up. This helped my mind connect to the message on a deeper level.

I was meditating every morning for anywhere between five and twenty minutes depending on how much time I had. I liked leaving the time frame open. If I had extra time, I meditated longer. If I overslept, I meditated for a shorter time. The important thing was that I continued the practice daily.

Affirmation
I observe a sense of peace,
washing over my body, mind & spirit.

As I come to know,
I am safe in this moment.

Repeat.

During silent meditations, it's useful to connect to a mantra. *Mantra* may sound intimidating, but it is simply using repeated words to enhance a specific focus, which shifts the frequency of your thoughts.

I was first introduced to mantra during a yoga teacher training in 2018, but wasn't fully able to connect to this practice until I found myself in a kundalini meditation studio in 2022. It was here that I started to learn and apply the concept of frequency and vibration.

At this point in time, I began to connect to the idea that my own words are a frequency of personal power. I already had an affirmation practice, but learning the concept of mantras elevated the work as I began to newly focus on sound as vibration to enhance my words.

The science of mantra is based on the idea that the universe is made of sound, sound is made of vibrations, and all matter is constructed from vibrating energy. This means that everything that exists, has its own vibrational frequency.

Sound familiar?

With this idea, you use your words to emit a specific frequency. When you speak, or think, words on a continuous basis, those words eventually become your truth and will begin to reframe your thoughts, and align you with positive frequencies that will attract positive outcomes. The purpose of this is to match the vibration you seek with your thoughts, so that the universe can meet that vibration and attract similar energy into your life.

Mantras, of any kind, can help lift your internal vibrations. Remember, when I say *meeting the vibrations (or frequency) of the universe*, I mean to project outwardly what you want to call into your own life. "What you project outwardly, will return to you." This is the power of the law of attraction *(thank you Abraham Hicks)*.

The one thing that has always been consistent on this journey are my affirmations. But similar to the ups and downs of life, some days I believe them and other days I struggle. Nothing is perfectly linear, including healing. There will always be challenges with new situations, new trauma, new heartbreak, new disappointment. Consistency will always be the key to long term healing and growth. I continue even when it's hard or when I don't feel like it. I continue even when I am half ass-ing the practice just to maintain the habit of doing it. I continue forward no matter what, because forward is the only way to go.

Affirmation
I observe.
I reflect.
I let go.

Self-regulation is all about feeling safe within yourself. When you feel safe, you can continue the road to personal growth with confidence and security. This sense of safety brings about peace and stability that is needed to achieve your goals. Safety makes you feel grounded. Safety makes you feel stable. Safety equals a strong, solid base, in which you can build upon and expand yourself higher.

Everyone's regulation process will look different. Some will practice breathing techniques, some will meditate, listen to music, take a bath or shower, some will exercise or go for a walk, and some people will use mantras or positive affirmations. Knowing what works best for you will help you to regulate faster and more efficiently.

The trick to beginning any type of new practice is to simply begin. Let go of expectations, let go of resistance and give it a try. Like anything else, don't stop if it becomes hard. Give yourself the opportunity to succeed, which in turn will give you the drive to continue. The biggest thing to remember is that you can achieve any goal that you set out to do, so give yourself a chance and don't give up before the miracle of change occurs.

Journal Prompts:

1. *Pick a set amount of time that you will practice meditation, and settle on a specific time of day to stay consistent (before bed or first thing in the morning is best). Find a guided meditation that you feel aligned with or use the affirmation/mantra in this chapter to repeat internally in a silent meditation. After you practice, journal how you felt or anything that came up for you.*
2. *How did this practice make you feel?*
3. *Did you find it difficult to turn off your mind?*
4. *Did anything specific come up for you?*
5. *Create a simple affirmation (one-three sentences) that is easy to remember. Begin to use it as a mantra, repeating it again and again until it becomes a true belief.*

Example: I am grateful for my life. I have everything I need. I am worthy of great things.

Chapter 8: Honesty

Affirmation

I am confident within the understanding of truth.

*I am secure within the freedom
of honesty.*

*I am faithfully connected to my words,
expressing responsibility through
the language of authenticity .*

It is so.

Honesty (noun)
hon·es·ty

    a: adherence to the facts : sincerity
    b: a refusal to lie, steal, or deceive in any way.

In the beginning of any journey, there is a place and time where self-honesty is essential. Honesty is such a tricky thing, because sometimes people don't even know when they may be lying to themselves. I believe it's a self-preservation habit, justifying and rationalizing behaviors and actions to feel better, but this often gets in the way of personal growth.

If you are willing to put in the work to step into your power and align with your true self, the lies need to go and honest admissions need to occur. But what does this mean? In a nutshell, no more excuses, no more blaming others, and fully accepting responsibility for your own life. This sounds simple, but believe me it takes some work. It begins with taking an honest look at yourself and the choices you have made up to this moment.

Most people will find it difficult to fully face themselves. It's much easier to try to escape from your thoughts and blame others, instead of accepting responsibility, in order to avoid reality. Believe me, I've done this. The obvious people to blame will be parents, ex-partners, close acquaintances, or better yet, personal rivals which oddly enough can be a sibling or best friend. The relationships you have with other people will and do play a role in how you react and behave in future experiences.

However, you are responsible for yourself. You are the only one who can change your behaviors.

Blaming others will never be conducive to this process. This means taking responsibility for the part you play in situations. Sorry to say this but YES, you always play some type of role. Don't fall into the victim mentality, it's not sexy for anyone. Step into the space of owning your own shit. This is the practice of honesty, self-awareness and acceptance.

Part of practicing honesty is observing. Because each person has a different perspective on what the truth is, and each situation has its own unique context, honesty can be relative. Think of the saying, "There are two sides to every story, and somewhere in between lies the truth." This means that each person views situations in a certain way that will be different from how other people see it. Something may be true to one person and take on an entirely different meaning to another.

So the question is, how do you decipher the truth, when there are so many different versions of it? It's simple, just focus your attention on your own motives, behaviors, and reactions. While observing any situation, ask yourself; *How did I act and why? Was it fear based? Do I have a motive? Am I trying to manipulate in order to get a specific outcome?*

Recognizing your own motives is important. In order to stay aligned with the energy of the universe, you must try to not manipulate the truth. Manipulation tells the universe that you do not trust the process. Releasing motives will help to ensure that you are in sequence with your vibrational energy and that it matches the energy of the universe.

Self-honesty can be hard. It is easy to get down on yourself for past mistakes. In this journey it is never helpful to dwell on the past. During your experience with identifying the lies, you also need to forgive. Forgiveness of the past and forgiveness of yourself is the ultimate expression of compassion and love. This is the energy that will help you continue to walk forward, towards your true self.

The more honest you are,
the more open,
the less fear you will have.
- Dalai Lama

In my own story, I have come face to face with the ugly truth of authentic honesty on many different occasions. I'll bring it back to early on in my journey when I needed to admit that my life was unmanageable, and I needed to make major changes in order to create a life worth living.

This is where I began. I was 26 years old. I had nothing to show for my life. I lived in my mother's basement. I lost numerous jobs throughout my early twenties. I had multiple speeding tickets on my drivers license that I was ignoring and hoping would magically go away. I didn't want to take responsibility for myself and my mistakes. I hid behind lies, excuses and justifications.

I often put blame on my childhood experiences, which definitely played a role, but I had to come to terms with the truth that it was my responsibility to work through my trauma. No matter how I was affected by my past, I was the one to blame for driving my life into the ground, and only I could be the one to fix it.

"If you only knew how hard my life was, you would understand why I can't change," was the biggest lie I would tell myself. I was living in a state of "poor me." This was all ego. The ego loves to blame and play victim. These excuses had to go, but the only way to do that was to admit that I needed help.

The honesty here was that I needed to change my life, or I was going to continue on living an empty existence. Naturally, this type of honesty brought up a lot of fear. Not only did I need to admit I needed help, I also had to be real about the wrongdoing I was taking part in for so many years.

When I entered recovery I had to learn how to be truthful with myself, and with others. It was very uncomfortable. I got so accustomed to lying as a defense mechanism that I had to practice this constantly. I came to see that the truth was not scary, it was actually freeing.

Eventually I was able to take responsibility for my life, no matter who was "at fault." This freedom gave me the opportunity to identify the changes that needed to occur within me in order to heal and grow. This was only the beginning of my journey with self-honesty. So much more has been revealed. So much inner work had to be done.

Affirmations to encourage self-confidence have helped me connect to my truth. Being honest with myself has helped me to become acquainted with who I am. When I know who I am, I know what I want for myself. And when I know what I want for myself, my goals become clear.

Affirmation
I am honest with myself.
I have compassion & forgiveness.
I honor truth.

Honesty takes courage because it can be uncomfortable, but within the truth of discomfort, is the potential of true and real personal growth. You are able to see clearly the exact nature of the situations in your life. With that clarity you can then begin to make better choices that are aligned with your desired future.

Remember, you are responsible for your own life. Being honest with yourself will steer the ship of your life in the right direction. It will help you take the reins, truly knowing who you are, where you are, and where you want to go.

Journal prompts:

1. *Where can you be more honest in your life?*
2. *Are you willing to make changes?*
3. *Where can you use honesty to help you move forward?*
4. *Create an affirmation including an honest admission of something you would like to release and/or forgive. Complete the affirmation with a loving statement to yourself.*

Example: I forgive myself for the internal lies that have kept me stuck. I lovingly open my mind and heart to the truth of acceptance.

Chapter 9: Self–Awareness

Affirmation

I am tuned in to awareness of self,
acknowledging areas of potential growth.

I am aligned with the healing powers of the universe,
connected to the energy that flows within.

I am honoring all aspects of me,
embracing my journey with
love & kindness.

It is so.

Self-awareness (noun)
self-aware·ness

: an awareness of one's own personality or individuality

With honesty, comes self-awareness. Once you come face to face with who you are and who you want to be, you now have the ability to make the necessary changes, and take the necessary actions needed for you to manifest the future you envision for yourself. This is crucial because you tend to be the very person who holds yourself back from your desired outcomes. With self-awareness, you can identify when you are living in fear and "see yourself" coming, before you make choices that can hinder your journey forward.

Let's look at the definition of self-awareness. This is the ability to see and understand your individual traits such as; emotions, actions, behaviors, beliefs, values, and thought patterns. This is helpful when embarking on any healing journey because once you understand how you tick, the better you can prepare yourself to push through uncomfortable situations, enabling you to grow as an individual.

In essence, awareness is a powerful tool that helps you identify your triggers, see specific behavior patterns, and regulate your emotions. In turn, this will help you choose appropriate reactions. If you are aware of yourself, you become aware of your triggers. This will help you find the reason behind the way you respond. When you can identify those reasons, you can be aware during future events and be able to act accordingly.

I can tell you for certain, awareness is a bitch, but also imperative in the process. It's hard because awareness is basically a self-analysis and usually occurs in the "not so pretty" moments. It's truly another form of self-honesty.

Knowing others is intelligence;
knowing yourself is true wisdom.
– Lao Tzu

My words can be a tool for creation, but have also served as a defense mechanism when feeling overwhelmed or unworthy. These feelings can be triggered by people, places, or things. If I had a dollar for every time I felt the need to tell someone "how it is" instead of just shutting my mouth, I'd be rich.

This stemmed from an insecurity of feeling unseen while I was growing up. Because of that feeling, I like to share my opinions, without being asked, and also in a manner that comes across as condescending. I dislike this quality in me so much that it is painful to be aware of it. However, without awareness there is no opportunity for improvement.

In my recovery journey, I became aware of this character trait early on. I had no filter when I allowed my emotions to take over. Fun fact, there is a very fine line between speaking your mind and being hurtful.

Today, one way I practice self-awareness is by trying to pause before speaking. I use the acronym "T.H.I.N.K." Before I speak, I try to ask myself;

"Is it true? Is it honest? Is it important? Is it necessary? Is it kind?"

I have an image of this saved as the homescreen on my phone for a constant reminder that I don't always have to say every thought that comes to mind. With self-awareness comes the ability to pause before reacting. This is the act of practicing discernment. It is the understanding, or comprehension, of what is necessary and what can be kept to myself.

It's hard to admit, but I am not always the victim in my life's circumstances. There are many times, usually due to my over opinionated mouth, where I have been the agitator.

I used to play victim to my ex-husband's sudden change of heart within our marriage but the truth is, I wasn't all sunshine and rainbows either. This was not an easy realization. When I began to see the role I played in my relationship, the awareness was jarring.

I had to admit to myself that I have tendencies to be controlling, manipulative, and judgmental. All of these unattractive qualities derive from my own insecurities and fears of outcomes not going my way.

I have identified a few facts. First, when I attempt to control, it creates a tension within the energy that actually makes things harder. Going with the flow isn't simple, but it does allow for peaceful mergence into what is happening, instead of a constant fight that causes anxiety and angst.

Second, anytime I try to manipulate in my favor, I usually experience great setbacks. I've seen this happen within forced relationships, as well as, trying to finagle my way into a position within my career. Anytime I didn't allow things to emerge without force, I never actually got what I wanted. When it wouldn't work out, I would then fall into a space of regret, shame, guilt, and sometimes even depression.

Being utterly aware of my behaviors enabled me to change, and freed me from resistance. I don't always need to be right. I don't always need to control or manipulate situations. I don't always need to say the first thing that comes to mind.

Affirmations have helped me throughout this process. When I see my character flaws arising, I try to let go of the old behavior by releasing it to the universe and then calling in the type of behavior I want to connect to. I would say words that would free me from control or judgment, and ask for patience and compassion in return.

Manifestation comes from easeful flow, and any tension that exists within the energy will only cause confusion. This is a continuous practice. I couldn't just say the words once and magically be cured. With affirmations, I was able to create trust in the universe, which loosened my grip and allowed the right energy to emanate.

Affirmation
I embrace self-awareness.
I am able to change what no longer serves me.
I am worthy of freedom from self.

Again, I will reiterate, awareness can be painful but it is the catalyst for change. Without the awareness of self, you may be naive to the destructive behaviors that are causing harm.

The process of self-reflection is challenging but it allows you to meet yourself in your true form. It removes the cloak of illusion and brings about a level of growth that some will never achieve. Utilizing affirmations will help to call in the qualities that you want to increase in your life, while letting go of the parts of yourself that only cause emotional pain.

Am I always perfect at this? Absolutely not! Awareness can often bring about discouragement when I realize the way I have been acting and identify that it does not align with who I want to be in this world. When I fall short, I can make amends, and try to do better next time.

Real healing takes courage and persistence. Self-awareness is taking responsibility for your own healing, so you may let go of the past and grow into the future. Healing gives you the opportunity to know yourself, to answer to your own conscience, and to own your part of things instead of blaming external forces. You can take responsibility and reap the rewards that come from being accountable for your actions. You are capable of feeling the whole range of human emotions while also facing life on life's terms in appropriate, kind, respectable ways. With this principle, you are continuing forward on the journey of meeting your authentic self and seeing a clear vision for your future.

Journal prompts:

1. *What are some character flaws or behaviors that you often act out on?*
2. *Are these actions aligned with who you want to be?*
3. *Were you acting out of fear?*
4. *How can you change these behaviors?*
5. *Write an affirmation that releases the old pattern and calls in the new behavior.*

Example: I release the urge to control. I am patient. I am calm. I am kind.

Chapter 10: Acceptance

Affirmation

I accept myself truly & fully,
honoring & loving all parts of me.

I accept others wholly & respectfully,
witnessing through a lens of
kindness & compassion.

I accept the absence of control,
focusing on the things that are within my own power to
adjust.

I shift into a space of ease,
believing that acceptance is calmness & calmness is
liberation.

It is so.

Accept (verb)

ac·cept

    a: to endure without protest or reaction
    b: to regard as proper, normal, or inevitable
    c: to recognize as true : believe

Acceptance as a whole is not easy but it is amazing when you can achieve it. In order to accept others, you first must accept yourself. This means you need to love and honor yourself in all facets; the good, the bad, the bright and the dark. Acceptance is growth. This is the culmination of honesty and awareness. This is you honoring who you truly are.

Not only is accepting oneself a big piece of the puzzle to clarify your own wants, needs and desires, it is also a way to help find peace in the moment. Accepting situations for what they truly are is something that cannot be overlooked when manifesting your intentions. Humans love to get lost in the mind, getting stuck in the "could have, should have, or would have been," thought process, easily becoming stuck in delusion or denial.

This usually occurs when there is a resistance to the truth of a situation, finding it hard to let go and move on. Moving on means change and change is scary. It is the unknown and the unfamiliar which can trigger the loop of "what ifs." *What if it doesn't work out? What if I fail? What if it's too hard or too lonely or too uncomfortable?*

The healing process is not consistent. Sometimes you may feel like you are going around a merry-go-round, until finally the pain is great enough, and you jump off the ride. Once you get off the loop of illusion and begin to step into the reality of acceptance, it takes some time to become grounded and see things clearly again.

There is often major denial or bargaining within the process of acceptance that keeps you from surrendering to the truth. This lack of letting go can result in repeating the same mistake over and over again, even against your better judgment. Trust me, I have found myself in this situation many times.

It can be tricky sometimes because you are raised with values and beliefs passed on to you by parents or guardians. The beliefs and values of those who raised you can then become your own values, or what you *think* to be your own values. Acceptance, at times, is coming to the realization of what beliefs are actually your own, and what beliefs are influenced by societal norms, family, relationships, and life experiences. Every opinion you hear, story that is told, or experience shared can have an affect on the values that you begin to hold in your own life. It is important to identify what is true for you, and not rely on other people's beliefs to determine your own.

Sometimes the acceptance of truth can be painful, but remember it cannot hurt you, so be gentle with yourself. The feelings of discomfort can be so raw, but feelings are not facts. Allow yourself to feel. Processing your feelings enables the growth and clarity that you'll need to accept and take action.

Acceptance can be a constant challenge. Some days it may be easy to let go, and other days may be filled with denial and resistance. Part of acceptance is giving yourself permission to not always be perfect. Accept that there are areas in life where you are strong and self-sufficient, and other areas that may still need work.

The truth is that you may be working on different aspects of your life forever, and that is a beautiful thing. Self-work fosters continuous growth and enhances internal wisdom. It also helps you continue to practice commitment when working towards your intentions. The only true constant in this lifetime is change, and your goals can, or will, change over time.

You are allowed to change your mind. You are allowed to make a decision and then go back and say it wasn't the right choice. That is acceptance. When you connect to acceptance, you connect to the truth of how things are, not what you believe them to be. Acceptance is taking off the rose colored glasses and seeing clearly. It is having the power to understand when something isn't working and accepting when things need to be adjusted or changed.

Coming to terms with honesty and acceptance is not easy by any means but it is the essence of letting go of the things that are holding you back. With acceptance you can begin to release the things that are not serving you. This begins the process of letting go and welcoming change into your life.

It's best to accept life as it really is
and not as I imagined it to be.
- Paulo Coelho

There are so many examples in my story that I can refer to when talking about acceptance. One that stands out the most is accepting the end of my marriage. This ending brought about a major learning experience, specifically in the realm of self-honesty and awareness.

I met my ex-husband in 2017, shortly after entering recovery. I was smitten with him immediately, that love at first sight type of energy. I fell for him because of his passion for learning and self-growth. It inspired me, especially at that point in my life when I was just starting to discover who I was and what I wanted.

This was my first serious relationship; the first person I lived with and the first person that I saw an actual future with. All the feelings were like a whirlwind of newness. I quickly fell into the fairy tale mindset, with all these hopes of the future and the belief that love would conquer all.

Unfortunately, somewhere within the relationship, misalignments began to become very apparent. Future goals and core values didn't match up, and turmoil started to creep in. But like any good dramatic love story, the two of us held on for dear life, pushing forward no matter the cost.

It's odd to say that I rushed into my marriage, especially since we were together for five years prior to becoming engaged. But despite that fact, there was a lack of acceptance that held us both hostage within our own denials.

Listen, I don't want to undermine my relationship with my ex. I would never speak an ill word against him. He is a great person with a big heart. However, not accepting the relationship for what it was kept me blind to all the signs screaming "STOP!"

I planned a beautiful wedding. It was an amazing day in July of 2022. The sun was out. I felt absolutely gorgeous in my bridal gown. I was surrounded by my family and excited to see my soon to be husband. It remains one of my favorite days. It was perfect. I felt that I finally arrived and I was on track for my future plans. But by September there were already problems in paradise, and by March of 2023, only nine months after "I do," we were planning to separate.

I was faced with a choice. Accept the reality of the situation, or continue on in my delusions that things *could* change.

Acceptance is hard. In theory, knowing the facts should make it easy, but for me not so much. I held onto the hope for my relationship for a long time. I couldn't let it go out of pure fear. Fear of change. Fear of the unknown. Fear of starting over.

The experience brought about more awareness, forcing me into a space of acceptance. I needed to begin to see the reality as it is, and not as I want it to be. I had to stop creating narratives in my head based on the potential I saw in people. I had to begin to accept people for who they are and situations for what they were.

Once I gained clarity, I could shift my focus to the changes that needed to occur in order to live my best life. During this time of healing, I used affirmations to help release my attachment to the past and increase my hope for the future.

This was the act of letting go and trusting the journey ahead. Within the space of acceptance, peace and joy can grow, ultimately embracing change without fear and increasing the power of manifestation.

Affirmation
I let go of attachment to outcome,
flowing into a place of allowance & acceptance,
trusting the path of my unfolding journey.

The amount of serenity in my life is equal to my amount of acceptance. Meaning, the more I can find acceptance in the present moment, the more peace I can find within myself. With this peace I can connect to the energy I am seeking to attract into my life and harness that energy into my desired future.

The process begins when you accept that you cannot control everything, but you can control your own actions, behaviors and choices. This is taking responsibility for your healing, your journey, and your patterns.

There are areas in life where acceptance may come easy and other areas where it does not. Accept you are a work in progress, and lean on affirmations to use words that will continuously solidify the truth of your own reality.

True acceptance is accepting yourself for who you are and loving yourself regardless, knowing that it is okay to fall short, it's okay to not know everything, and it's okay to change your mind. The responsibility lies within the acknowledgement and the awareness of the areas that need work.

Acceptance is where you can begin to open your mind to new perspectives that can bring about the most beautiful changes that you may never have dreamed of.

Journal prompt:

1. *What is something that you are working on accepting in your life?*
2. *Is this acceptance being blocked by a false belief?*
3. *How would your life be different if you were able to fully accept this truth?*
4. *Create an affirmation of acceptance, releasing any attachment you may have to a false narrative or belief.*

Example: I let go of the fear of loneliness. I accept myself as I am in this moment. Whole, Loveable, and Free

Chapter 11: Release Self–Doubt

Affirmation

I courageously walk through self-doubt, connected to my confidence & self-assurance.

I align myself with the clarity of truth, fully free to feel safe within my own journey.

I am brave & I am worthy.

It is so.

Self-doubt (noun)

: a lack of faith in oneself : a feeling of doubt or uncertainty about one's abilities, actions, etc.

Self-doubt can occur, and keep recurring, throughout your life. How you deal with the feeling is what makes all the difference. Awareness that you are experiencing self-doubt is the first step. Identifying the trigger that sparks the doubt is next. Then comes affirmations of positive reassurance. These are powerful reminders that the self-doubt you are experiencing is a lie you are telling yourself out of a fear of failure.

Fear of failure is so common. It is almost a right of passage in the human experience, *especially* among people who are going against the grain, and walking the path to healing. The truth is, the mind is tricky. It will lie to you. It will convince you that "you cannot," when in reality, "you can." This can be a debilitating feeling but can also be shifted with the practice of positive self-talk.

If you doubt yourself, you're blocking your own ability to achieve what you set out to do. Self-doubt is a feeling, and feelings are not facts. Just because you have an insecure thought, does not mean you need to believe it, or let it dictate your behavior. Shift the perspective. Change the internal narrative. Remind yourself who you are and what you are capable of.

Doubt kills more dreams than failure ever will.
Believe in yourself. Never quit.
- David Crow

I myself experience fear and self-doubt often. It hinders my ability to make decisions, feel confident within myself, and believe in the goals I am working to achieve.

Identifying what is causing the doubt can be extremely helpful. *Is it failure? Is it rejection? Abandonment? Judgment?*

Usually, it's one of these core fears that's causing inaccurate thoughts to blur the mind. Coming back to the practice of positive self-talk will clear away the untruths you are telling yourself, allowing you to release the negative energy and return to the positive.

Holding space for others, whether in a classroom, yoga studio, or seminar, can bring me to a place of serious imposter syndrome.

In my second year teaching, I was asked to co-create a professional development seminar for a conference day at my school district. This session was titled "Yoga and Mindfulness for Health and PE," and was only available for my specific department, health and physical education.

At first I was honored to be able to hold space for my coworkers, but then I was almost paralyzed with fear.

"Who do I think I am?"

"I don't know what I'm talking about?"

"What if they figure out I'm a fraud?"

These were the thoughts that ran on repeat while attempting to put together my plans. I've been here before, so I knew the internal comments were not the truth. Anytime I hold any type of informational workshop, the same questions come to mind. It is like insecurity on steroids.

The first thing I did for my presentation was make a slide about who I am. Simply getting started unintentionally began to build my self-esteem. The original intention was to introduce myself as the speaker, but it turned into much more. It was a reminder that I did in fact have the qualifications to be teaching the concepts that were being presented.

I started by listing my experience in the content area, as well as certifications that I have earned. Writing and reading my own credentials acted as a sort of "I am me" affirmation during this process.

In the end, I held my head high during the presentation and got through it with grace and integrity. It reminded me of my own worth, and served as a confidence boost that I needed more than I knew. I simply had to remember who I was in order to fight off the self-doubt.

Walking through the discomfort of doubt isn't always easy. Any endeavor might leave you feeling like it's pointless to start because of possible failure. In moments of hesitation, continue to tell yourself who you are. Take a breath and listen to the messages around you. The signs can come from yourself, a friend, or even a feeling of intuition.

A friend of mine once told me, "Every single time it's been okay, it's going to be okay this time too." He said this during a moment of pure resistance. I was about to submerge myself into an ice bath, something I've done hundreds of times prior, but this time my mental and emotional state was elevated with fear. I was going through a period of growth that was causing discomfort and resulting in major self-doubt of my capabilities, both physical and mental.

When I heard the words, I took it both literally and figuratively. Clearly he was referring to the freezing cold ice bath that I was about to enter in the dead of winter, and how each time I've done this practice before I've lived to tell the tale. But I also took it as a validating statement that I was going to survive my feelings as well. I've done so in the past, countless times before. Each time being difficult, but each time coming out on the other side stronger and wiser.

I often reflect on the fact that I have faced self-doubt on so many occasions. When I got clean from substances, when I went back to school, when I went to interviews, when I started new jobs, and when I ended relationships. If I listened to the false thoughts that were circulating my mind at any point in time, I wouldn't be where I am today; clean, master's degree, a teacher, and now a published author.

Affirmation
I am worthy.
I am capable.
I am safe.
All is well.

It is so essential to understand the depths of your perceptions. You may perceive things to be true in your mind, when they are in fact false. The thought of "I can't" is *always* a lie. You are capable of achieving anything you set out to do. This consistent belief will keep the energy moving forward.

This is a reminder. Whether it's a break up, job change, loss of any kind, or doing something that pushes you past your comfort zone; if through all other obstacles everything ended up being okay, why would this time be different?

Identify the times you made it through challenges, regardless of self-doubt, to remember *you are safe*. Continuously affirm yourself by saying, "all will be well." You've been through trials before, life is filled with them, but you're still standing, aren't you? Even if an experience was troubling, the positive is that you've made it to the other side. You pushed yourself to conquer your fear and doubt. You pushed yourself to heal and grow. That shit is magic.

You have the choice to change your thinking and align with positive self-talk. When you release self-doubt, you fall into the flow of allowance and trust, unattached to a specific outcome, and free from the illusion of control.

Journal Prompt:

1. *What are your core fears and where do they stem from?*
2. *How have they caused you to doubt yourself?*
3. *How have they held you back in the past?*
4. *Create an affirmation to release doubt by releasing the narrative of fear and remind yourself of your power.*

Example: I let go of my fear of inadequacy. I am capable of creating great things.

Chapter 12: Unlocking Independence

> **Affirmation**
>
> *I am released from the cage of resistance,*
> *allowing myself to open the door to connection & hope.*
>
> *I embrace the journey of transformation,*
> *allowing myself to be in the energy of peace & calm.*
>
> *I align with trust in the unfolding,*
> *stepping into a space of pure freedom to choose me.*
>
> *It is so.*

Freedom (noun)

free·dom

   : the quality or state of being free: such as

   a: the absence of constraint in choice or action

   b: independence

   c: unrestricted

Freedom is the purpose of the soul. It's the calling of the spirit. It's peace within the heart. Freedom equals inner peace and inner peace is the structure of ease and grace. This feeling of ease is the concept of allowance and in the energy of allowance is the space for creation.

Throughout my journey, my soul has craved the true meaning of what it is to be peaceful, to truly and fully live in the space of ease. Freeing myself from limiting beliefs was vital. My purpose was to find the freedom to choose myself.

In order to become the ultimate creator of your life, the ability to validate yourself is so essential. The only way to truly manifest your desires is to believe in yourself. This belief will take you to the next level. To truly believe is to have the ability to affirm yourself, which is a fucking superpower.

My lack of belief in myself was always a huge roadblock. I constantly needed approval. I needed to control situations to ensure my own emotional well-being. I needed people to build my sense of worth. All of this *need* was very chaotic, tense, unstable energy. The exact opposite of peace.

Calm energy allows things to flow easier. Tense energy creates resistance. When unlocking my independence, I learned that peace was the formula for success. Belief is a concept that brings peace. I had to believe that I could be free from fear, doubt, and anger. I was the prison guard of my own restriction, and I had the key to the cage that I was locked in.

Affirmations were my savior. Each helped me to continue to let go of the past and trust in the future. Each helped me to build a belief in myself. Each helped me to feel safe within my body, mind and heart. I used affirmations to cultivate new beliefs about myself to build the freedom I longed for. I no longer wanted to be stuck.

In order to become free, I first needed to find out how I got trapped in the first place. I needed to figure out where it all began. Unlocking independence begins with unlocking the past, which is the practice of honesty, awareness, and acceptance.

While writing the pages of this book, I started to create a timeline. I got the idea from, *Forgiving What You Can't Forget*, by Lysa Terkeurst. I was going through a spiritual crisis and was seeking ways to heal myself from all the trauma that I've endured in my life up to this point. It was through deep self-reflection, and the help of the teachings within Terkeurst's work, where I found the secret of true freedom. *Observe. Reflect. Let go. Forgive.*

Letting go gives us freedom,
and freedom is the only condition for happiness.
- Thich Nhat Hanh

So here it is. The prologue of my childhood. I share this in hopes that you find the inspiration to explore your own past, not to dwell in it, but to ultimately heal it. Within reflection comes understanding, compassion, forgiveness, and liberation.

Bear with me, this might take some time.

Firstly, I always found safety and comfort from my Dad. I had a contentious relationship with my mother, so it was only fitting that I naturally found solace with my dad. We were very close when I was growing up. Before my parents divorced it was notably clear who I was more comfortable with. After their divorce, I had the strong urge to fill a caretaker role for my dad since he was going to be living alone (codependency*). I remember being so worried that he wasn't going to be able to take care of himself. Before we left my childhood home to move into my mom's new house, I wrote directions for how to do laundry and left them on top of the dryer, just to make sure he would know how to do it. I recall so vividly taking on his emotions, or what I assumed his emotions were (another codependent trait). I felt it was my responsibility to make sure he was going to be okay.

During this time I felt very unstable. We were constantly moving between two homes. Half the week at my dad's and half the week at my mom's. This lack of stability at home created more uneasy energy within me. This is where my need for control was amplified. I felt so out of control and I craved stability so deeply that I soon learned to manipulate people in order to create a sense of security in my life. This habit would continue well into my adult years.

In this transition, I leaned heavily on my relationship with my dad because it gave me a purpose and made me feel needed and important. Within the first year, both of my parents found new partners. My father started dating a woman who was in her late twenties, and at first I loved and welcomed the friendship that I had with her. She had a sense of emotional sensitivity towards me that was always lacking in other relationships.

When I was 14 years old, my father got engaged. It was an odd feeling for me. While I did love my soon-to-be stepmother,

I was overwhelmed with fear and jealousy. They asked me to announce to the family that they were engaged. This memory is burned into my brain. I was at my Aunt's house and the whole family was there. When it was time to make the announcement, I stood in the kitchen filled with anxiety. I said the words out loud and then cried. I did not know it at the time, but looking back as an adult, I can see that I was beginning to feel replaced. I felt a lot of fear about what my relationship with my father would look like now that he had a new woman in his life to take care of him.

They married and soon after my stepmother was pregnant. I don't have full recollection of this but I am told that I was very mean to her during her pregnancy. We were expecting a new sister and although there was excitement within me, I was also projecting a lot of anger and sadness towards everyone around me. This is about the time that I started to get into trouble, hanging out with the *bad* crowd and dabbling with drugs.

When my younger sister came into the world, I was 15 and again confused with conflicting emotions of excitement and jealousy. There were now two new women in my Dad's life and I felt irrelevant and unimportant.

Now, I do not hold any resentment or blame towards my father. Although we spent many years during this time estranged and distant, we healed our relationship and are very close today. It was not his fault that he wanted to move forward in his life after his divorce and find his own place of love and belonging with a partner. This story is about me and how I perceived and dealt with everything, and how it shaped my relationship with men going forward.

There I was. A teenager with trust issues, emotional dysregulation, jealousy, and feeling completely exposed and unsafe. So, it is no surprise that I sought safety from a man, as I did in my early childhood years. I met my first boyfriend and was immediately drawn to a few things. I remember the first time I saw him. He was smoking a cigarette, which excited me because I was knee deep in the beginning stages of my rebellion.

This was the first of four major relationships in my life. All of which had different levels of toxicity. My high school boyfriend introduced me to a lifestyle of trouble. The relationship fueled my desire to act out and take risks. It also played a role in exacerbating my abandonment wound. He died in a car accident when I was 17, which left me feeling alone and left behind. Of course death is not intentionally leaving, but I felt that way nonetheless. I didn't handle this well at all, rightfully so. I turned to harder drugs and promiscuous emotional fulfillment from men.

In my college years, I entered the next extremely passionate but toxic relationship. This was the most outwardly obviously horrendous relationship that I have ever been exposed to, besides what you would see on TV and in the movies. We were together from freshman year until the beginning of our senior year. The whole experience was filled with booze, epic fights, and lustful make-ups. It was abusive to say the least. It all came abruptly to an end one night that left me in the hospital with a concussion and him in jail for assault and battery.

Soon after he was shipped off to rehab, never to return to school, leaving me once again to feel left behind, abandoned, and alone. It must sound weird to some people, how I would feel that way after being a part of a relationship like that. But that's the nature of toxic relationships. The codependency beats you down to believing you aren't worth having more, so when you are left with nothing, it's as if your whole life is turned upside down.

My next relationship began when I was 23. He was about nine years older than me and we met in a rehab facility. Yes, I know, the perfect place to begin a romance (eye-roll). This experience pulled me deeper into the world of drugs. We were together for about two years. There was so much chaos. I began to lose myself. I gave up on dreams. I compromised my morals and values. I became estranged from my family. I must say, I was in love with the lifestyle. Acting out became a part of my personality. It was as if I wore a badge of honor everytime I participated in "bad girl" behavior. But, as with all risks, living this way had significant consequences and ended with an overdose that took his life.

Last, but certainly not least, my ex-husband. We met at a gym about seven months after I got clean in recovery. I was starting to pull my life back together and finally realign myself with goals and aspirations for my future. I think you all get the gist of this story by now. Love at first fight. Fast paced relationship. Ignored the red flags. Forced the continuation and progression of the partnership. Extreme denial. And an ultimate ending. This ending was his choice. He left in June 2023 and I was completely and utterly shattered.

Within all of these life lessons, the common theme is the same. Whether I was left by death, the law, or the most hurtful, by choice, I felt completely abandoned, alone and confused, always asking the same questions; *Why? What was the pattern? Why did I need to experience such pain? Where did I go wrong?* I put a lot of blame on myself. I needed to find the answers to become free from my suffering, and ultimately the choices that kept leading me to the same ending.

Freedom is within the truth of open and honest self-reflection. Freedom is the act of letting go. While processing all the events of my life, I was able to identify the patterns and begin to understand myself more. You cannot heal if you bury and ignore the past. The healing work is in your experiences.

Once you are free from the past and are able to work through the trauma to truly heal, you will begin to increase your belief.

Believing that you can heal will in turn enhance the level of your healing. Believing in yourself will elevate your freedom, leading you to be liberated from judgment, obsession, and self-doubt.

Affirmation
I embrace the past.
I embrace change.
I embrace the unknown.

I now invite you to free yourself from your past by facing it head on. Observe the timeline, the facts, and the experiences. Reflect on the relationships, the trauma, and the feelings. Acknowledge all the *things*, and then allow yourself to forgive and let go. No more hiding, no more avoiding. Within the freedom of letting go, you give yourself the chance to heal. Allow yourself to change the narrative. Release the *control* that the past has held on you, and openly step into a future of peace.

Change is freedom from the past. It is growth and movement forward. This is the transformation that will bring peace and calmness into your world. This gentle energy is the space where you can connect to your power, believe in yourself, and manifest all the things that your mind dreams and your heart desires.

Journal prompt:

1. *Take a moment to reflect on your past. How does the past affect your current reality?*
2. *Can you identify any specific patterns that are recurring and keeping you stuck?*
3. *How can you make changes to release yourself from these patterns?*
4. *Create an affirmation to enhance your self-worth and confidence.*

Example: I have learned from my past, but it does not define me. I am brave, beautiful, and bold in the presence of this moment.

Codependency is a psychological condition that appears in relationships where a person has an unhealthy attachment to another.

Section Three
"I Affirm."

The Mind.

Affirmation

I am home within myself;
affirmed, grounded, & strong.

I am free from obsession of the mind;
balanced, secured, & focused.

I am grateful for clarity in this moment;
centered, connected, & clear.

It is so.

Now that you have met yourself through the practices of honesty, awareness, and acceptance, you can begin to understand how and why you see things in a certain light.

"Mind over matter" is a real thing! Just because humans are creatures of habit, does not mean you are destined to be stuck in old ways of thinking forever. Fresh perspectives allow you to continue to grow. If you consciously begin to shift your thoughts, you can ultimately begin to mold your mind with new thought patterns, leading to a new way of life.

Before manifesting, developing mental clarity is crucial. Mental clarity comes from the connection of the mind and body. It is the state of being where you're able to think clearly, focus intentions, and make secure decisions with confidence and courage. Feeling safe helps to calm the mind and bring about clarity. When you feel safe within your body, you then feel safe within your mind.

The mind is 95% subconscious thoughts. That means you are literally only consciously aware of about 5% of your thinking. Because of this fact, the brain tends to work on autopilot, choosing the neuro pathways that are most familiar. This is how thinking becomes habitual. The way to break the habit is to practice mindful thinking, ground yourself within your physical body, utilize affirmations to shift perspectives, and begin to take action.

Chapter 13: Opening Your Mind

> **Affirmation**
>
> *I open my mind to endless possibilities,*
> *ready to receive the gifts of the unknown.*
>
> *I wholeheartedly embrace acceptance,*
> *trusting all is unfolding for my highest potential.*
>
> *I free myself from the fear of change,*
> *having confidence & hope for all that*
> *is to come.*
>
> *It is so.*

Open-minded (adjective)

open-mind·ed

: receptive to arguments, new ideas or different perspectives

How do you open your mind?

It seems like a simple concept, but opening the mind is often met with a lot of resistance. Human beings can get stuck in learned behaviors that create patterns within the brain, forming a path of least resistance. Meaning, thoughts and behaviors become habitual, automatically following the recognized sequence of thinking, even if it's a behavior that is not necessarily *good*, or constructive.

Rumination is a continual pattern of negative thinking. The mind gets caught in repeated loops developed from past experiences, a.k.a. *schemas*. When people experience something that is perceived as negative, the brain will automatically go to that thought, whenever you experience a similar situation.

A "closed mind" is really speaking to the resistance to changing these patterns because your experiences have shaped the way your brain works. But, just like any habit that is formed, thought patterns can be healed and improved with the practice of opening your mind to different ideas.

Close-mindedness comes from familiar comfort. The saying, *get comfortable being uncomfortable*, is so relevant to personal growth. Humans become content with patterns because they have a "known outcome." This can be processed better than the "unknown," even if the known outcome is negative. When you know, or think you know what will happen, it is easier for your brain to fall into a thought pattern of familiarity, than it is to compute the endless possibilities that *could* happen.

Some believe in the concept of *unlearning98* behaviors. I believe you are never really unlearning anything. It's a process of *relearning*. With awareness and acceptance, you are able to identify defective thinking within yourself that does not align with your core values. The identification allows you to see what behaviors need to be shifted. You aren't really forgetting, or unlearning, anything. You are rewiring your brain to react differently. Truthfully, your initial thoughts may never change. The point is to see yourself coming and adjust accordingly, before you fall into the same old course of action.

So, how do you rewire the old ways of thinking and get comfortable with the unknown? Shift the mind to new perspectives. Having a closed mind is living in ego, thinking that your way is the best, or only way, to see and think. It is imperative to become open, to take suggestions, and to hear different points of view. This is releasing the ego mindset. Once you are able to begin exploring new ideas, you can then begin to adjust your thoughts.

> *Those who can't change their minds,*
> *can't change anything.*
> - George Bernard Shaw

For years I did things my way, continuously leading myself down a destructive path, even in recovery. I struggled with battling the expectations of what my life "should look like." What I have learned is that high expectations can come with major disappointment.

After my divorce, I began to panic. I felt that I was *behind*. Like I was running out of time. I began to get so desperate to not be single, that I continuously tried to fill the void with anyone who was available to me.

I was at a point where my idea of a relationship was what I like to describe as *"insert man here."* I was so focused on specific outcomes that I was trying to make anything fit, despite all clear red flags. My mind was closed.

At the age of 35, just under two years after my divorce, I was in a state of full anxiety over being alone and single. I just ended a relationship that lasted about three months and I was devastated at the failure. I carelessly attempted to make it work because I wanted to continue on the path towards where I thought I would be at this age.

My hyper-focus on relationships, children, and aging was ultimately closing me off to any other possible outcome for my future. I couldn't see the big picture. I lost all patience and I wanted what I wanted now (actually yesterday). A close friend of mine used an analogy that really unlocked my mind.

She said, "All you see is purple. All you want is purple. All you are focused on is purple. You aren't allowing yourself the opportunity to see the full rainbow."

I was so focused on specific outcomes, that I was completely closed off to any other possibility. I was continuously trying to force things in order to create the "picture perfect" life. All this did was create chaos and consequences, leaving me in mental and emotional pain. I needed to begin to open my mind to the possibility of my future not unfolding exactly how I once pictured it.

This internal struggle brought me to acceptance. I could not force any particular outcome. Things don't always have to go as planned. I believed that if everything went my way, I would be happy. Today, I try to see new perspectives and allow myself to be open to different realities, where my happiness can align with different opportunities.

I still continuously work on rewiring the thought patterns of "what my life should look like" with the use of positive self-talk, allowing my mind to welcome the idea of something different. I use the practice of affirmations to help guide me, focusing on open-mindedness, patience, and trust in the process.

Affirmation
I let go of attachment to the past.
I release expectations for the future.
I am open to new experiences,
embracing the excitement of the unknown.

The brain is a "pattern seeker," a creature of habit. Being comfortable within familiarity can make people very uneasy when faced with unknown possibilities. In order to get out of your own way and reroute your thoughts, it's helpful to turn off overthinking and find clarity.

You cannot force clarity. Sometimes you need to have your own experiences to figure out what it is you want. And guess what? That is opening the mind and accepting the unfolding exactly the way it is supposed to be, without force and without control.

As Yung Pueblo said, "Your initial reaction is usually your past trying to impose itself on your present." Let go of past thoughts and open the mind, so you may act differently in the presence of now.

Continuous use of positive affirmations will eventually create a new pattern of thinking to ease your mind into a space of openness and readiness to embrace new opportunities. Moving into the next chapters of this book, perspective, action, and willingness will be key players as you continue forward on the path of freedom.

Journal prompt:

1. *Where do you see pattern thinking in your life?*
2. *Can you identify the experiences that created these patterns?*
3. *Do these patterns hold you back from new experiences and opportunities?*
4. *Create an affirmation to help open your mind and trust the process.*

Example: I let go of thoughts that no longer serve me. I open my mind to new ideas.

Chapter 14: Shifting Perspectives

"

Affirmation

I shift my perspective,
seeing the truth of distorted thinking.

I am aware of my thoughts,
freeing my mind of old patterns & beliefs.

I release the illusion of control,
trusting the path to endless possibilities.

It is so.

"

Perspective (noun)

per·spec·tive

> **a:** a mental view or prospect
>
> **b:** the capacity to view things in their true relations or relative importance

Perspectives are individual to each person. I'm sure you've run into those who tend to have a negative outlook on life. Have you noticed that those people are usually surrounded by a lot of negativity? Evidence of the law of attraction. What you speak into the universe is what you attract into your life.

It is essential to be mindful of your words, consciously using a vibrational frequency that matches what you want to call into reality. Focusing on what you want, instead of what you don't want, helps the brain shift perspectives to positive outcomes. The use of affirmations and a practice of gratitude are good exercises to welcome fresh perspectives, create new patterns, and ultimately transform your whole view on life.

With a positive mind, you can more easily and gracefully achieve your goals. Awakening to the possibility of a different perspective, opens the potential to a deeper connection of honesty and acceptance, and helps to clear any blurred vision.

Take a moment to think about a certain situation in your life where your perspective may be negative. Ask yourself if the narrative you are speaking is in fact true, and if you can accept a new way of thinking in order to transform your thoughts from negative to positive. Changing the internal narrative with the use of affirmations is such an amazing tool to utilize.

Shift your mind from pessimistic thinking by being aware of yourself and your current patterns.

Do you complain?

Do you think bad things will always happen?

Do you feel you are doomed to fail?

If so, train your brain to stop by calling in the opposing thought of the positive result. If you complain often, focus on gratitude. If you think bad things will happen, focus on the possible optimistic outcomes. If you feel you are doomed to fail, practice affirmations of self-worth. All of these shifts in thinking will change the conversation in your brain.

Chart of Opposing Principles

Fear	Faith
Doubt	Courage
Hate	Love
Anger	Happiness
Sadness	Joy
Denial	Acceptance

Shifting perspectives also coincides with the practice of awareness and acceptance. When you get used to a certain situation in your life, you become complacent, even if it's uncomfortable or holding you back. When practicing awareness, and seeing the honest truth, you can open your mind to a new point of view and therefore open your life to new opportunities. In this state you can make decisions that are good for you, even if they may be hard, and even if you're filled with fear.

A shift in perspective opens a completely new set of unlimited possibilities.
- Satsuki Shibuya

I've often found myself in the head space of negative thinking. I can be extremely rigid, stuck in the perspective of my way being the best way, causing resistance to any other belief. This isn't always because I feel I am right and everyone else is wrong. Attempting to control outcomes is very much a defense mechanism to create an idea of security. I needed to accept this truth to be able to loosen the grip and shift my inner dialogue from fear to faith.

Control does not actually exist. You cannot control anything outside of your own emotions and behaviors. You are only in control of your own actions. If you think about it, there is a very small percentage of things that you can actually be in charge of. Everything else is out of your hands. However, many people attempt to maintain the thought that they can change outcomes in order to make themselves feel better.

This is a hard narrative to break. The illusion of control creates a feeling of safety. It is a response to fear of the unknown. I suffer from fear often. Fear has always held me back from being able to see clearly. Fear would drive me to the point of pure insanity, attempting to will things into my life, in order to feel like I was in the driver's seat.

How is fear based thinking created? In my story, my past experiences developed a sense of lack, causing me to become obsessed with the past and the future, completely neglecting the present.

Overly focusing on the past is how resentments are born. Overthinking the future is where fear begins to live. Not being present in the moment is how anger for what you "don't have" is created.

During my first teaching position, I experienced the need to shift my perspective. I was stuck in a very negative mindset every morning when I had to drive an hour, in very aggressive rush hour traffic, to work a job that I was not happy at. I found myself trying to control everything around me as an attempt to cope. I became overly judgmental, extremely opinionated, and had a condescending attitude that was causing harm in my relationships.

The reason I felt such anger and disappointment was directly related to the lack of acceptance for my past. When I was in school, I had a vision of where I wanted to be after I completed the program, and I wanted that vision to be created immediately. This is a common cycle that I would find myself in, resenting the past and all the "wasted" time I spent doing nothing but getting into trouble.

Each day I had resentment, anger, and fear. I didn't know how long I could continue to work in a place that felt toxic and unsupported. The whole reason I decided to change careers was to find a job where I felt joy and passion. The reality in the moment was not aligned with what I dreamt.

I had to shift the narrative. The internal dialogue in my mind was focused on the bad, making me feel completely out of control. I had two options, continue to feed the negative mind, or surrender the illusion of control to find peace.

This concept did not come easy. I struggled for many years to be able to open my mind to different perspectives. Truthfully, I can regress at any moment. Consistency with affirmations, brings me back to center, allowing my thoughts to flow easefully.

First, I had to let go of the resentment I was harboring for my past choices, I came to a place of acceptance. Without all my past experiences, I might not have known that I wanted to become a teacher. The path to education was created when I was introduced to recovery. Without all the craziness that led me there, I might not have ended up where I was, working towards a career that I was proud of.

The next step was to release my anger and frustration for the present circumstances. I needed to connect to love and gratitude.

I was lucky to even have a full time position with zero teaching experience. I started this job two weeks after completing my master's program, and most of the people I graduated with were still looking for positions. I needed to be thankful for the opportunity to gain experience and for my willingness to put in the effort, even when it was uncomfortable and unpleasant.

Lastly, I had to let go of my fear of the future. I was overwhelmed with the thought that it would never get better, creating a fear based mentality that ultimately blocked me from hope and faith. I needed to trust in the fact that situations always change. I had to lean into continued positive thinking, knowing I would eventually attract new opportunities. When fear is lifted, I am able to free myself from the negative thought pattern, shift the perspective, and make clear decisions that are good for my life.

After I went through the process of shifting perspective, I was able to identify what I could control; building my resume, applying for jobs, and putting in the work. I have found that when I align with acceptance, I can find more peace in the moment and eventually all works out beautifully. When I try to force a specific outcome, the energy is fractured and I end up being disappointed. When I release the illusion of control and negative thinking, I am able to connect to acceptance and faith and see a clear vision of my future.

In the end, I only spent six months at this job. Eventually, I found my next stepping stone as a temporary teacher at a more fitting school. This was still not exactly what I wanted, but I continued to use affirmations to connect to acceptance, love and faith. In turn, allowing me to continue my journey forward without resentment, anger or fear.

Affirmation

I choose to change my perspective.
I feel into the space of trust.
I connect to the faith of acceptance.

Perception can be riddled with illusion and self-deception. It can be clouded and distorted by fearful emotion. Stop and observe the reality of all things before getting fixated on outcomes. Connecting to stillness can help you see through the haze and into a clear reflection of truth. Freeing yourself from false narratives, and releasing the obsession of the mind, can deepen your insight and bring about a more positive outlook.

Shifting perspectives is an eye opening experience. It allows you to view life from a new lens of gratitude and clarity, creating space for you to become confident within your choices. This will help you to develop a clear vision for yourself. With a clear vision, aligned with positive values, you can begin to step into the power of creation.

Journal prompt:

1. *Do you experience any negative thought patterns in your life?*
2. *How can you shift your perspective and focus on gratitude?*
3. *Create an affirmation, using the chart above, to release the negative and call in the opposing positive energy.*

Example: I release my fearful thinking and connect to faith and trust in my process.

Chapter 15: Choice

Affirmation

I allow myself to let go,
creating space for faith & love.

I embrace the beauty of my life,
opening my world to an abundance
of gratitude.

I attract the energy I am seeking
to receive,
calling in unlimited opportunities.

I choose peace. I choose calm. I
choose me.

It is so.

Choice (noun)

: the act of choosing : selection

Being honest is a choice.
Acceptance is a choice.
Opening your mind to new ideas is a choice.
Pausing before you react is also a choice. Practicing detachment is a choice. Changing your mind is a choice. And giving into your feelings IS a choice.

You always have the opportunity to choose peace. You always have the opportunity to avoid conflict and negativity, and to align yourself with love and harmony. It does take courage to walk away from the things that don't benefit your life, but regardless of the difficulties, it's your decision to do so.

Self-confidence will help you prioritize your peace and happiness on a daily basis. This means choosing what's right for you despite what other people think or feel. This confident energy will also help to guide you when you may need to adjust the choices that you've already made. Nothing is final, and you are allowed to change your mind. New information may come to light that will affect your view about an original choice. And - THIS IS OKAY! In a world of infinite possibilities, how can you settle on one thing all the time?

In all moments of your life you have a choice. And yes I mean all moments, like every single day. You get to choose how your day is going to go, regardless of what events occur or what annoyances may arise.

Don't believe me? Let's take a look.

You can choose to let someone piss you off. You can choose to let something ruin your day. Or you can choose peace, and choose to be happy no matter what else is going on around you.

How? By releasing attachment to situations.

Detaching from other people's bullshit is exactly how you can remain in a state of peace and positive energy. Remember you attract the energy you are projecting, therefore you're protecting your own energy when you avoid the things that trigger negativity within you.

This isn't always easy. Practice by using affirmations to rewire your thoughts when you begin to feel agitated by the day to day frustrations. This will free you from the intrusive thought of hostility, and redirect your mind to a new pattern of thinking.

Changing your reactive thought patterns will enhance your connection to the power of your own choices. When you begin to see that you always have the option to reject the bad thoughts and choose to remain in your peace, you'll be able to calm the nervous system and clear the mind. This reinforces confidence in the choices you make for yourself.

It's important to listen to your heart and to feel into what is right for you. Your intuition won't lie. When you are connected to your inner peace, free from doubt, the heart will be your guide. This is the power of remembering that you have the ability to make your own choices, no matter what outside circumstances are occurring.

Choices are your own to make. Not for anyone else to decide. Your choices can be fluid and change at any moment. Choices can be scary, often leaving you wondering if it was *right* or *wrong*. Release that mentality and surrender to the experience that is the journey of your life. There is no "right or wrong." Nothing is a *mistake*. Every choice is simply an opportunity for lessons learned, which always leads to growth.

When making choices, take a pause and reflect on these questions. *Do I have a choice? What are my options? Do any of these options align with my wants, needs and goals? Do I feel confident in my decision? Did any new information come to light after the decision was made? Is this choice working?*

Make a practice of consciously choosing your words, and then notice how much energy and spirit you have, how others change around you, and how quickly you get things done.
- Dr. Shanti Shanti Kaur

A dear friend of mine always reminds me that, "Happiness is a choice."

I chose to get clean.

I chose to go back to school.

I consistently choose to exercise. To do my morning routine everyday. To go to work. And to nurture my relationships.

I could have chosen to do nothing, to change nothing, or work towards nothing. I could have chosen over and over again to stay in my comfort zone or to give into my own fears and doubts.

But I chose to build a life. I chose to show up. I chose to walk into the unknown. I continuously choose to push myself into a growth mindset. And I chose to create a life of happiness and joy.

Now, choices don't always go as planned. I chose to marry my husband, and I had to be brave enough to choose myself when it was time to walk away.

The courage to make choices for myself has always come from the fortitude to walk through fear. How? By releasing expectations.

Expectations of myself.

Expectations of others.

And expectations of society.

I needed to stop putting unrealistic expectations on myself and others. I needed to let go of the assumption of judgment. I needed to accept the fact that it doesn't matter what other people think. At the end of the day, only I live with my choices, therefore only I can make them.

Everyday is a decision to choose happiness. Even when things aren't going your way. Happiness IS a choice.

I can mindfully choose to free myself from overthinking and stress. I get to choose to align myself with the energy of peace and calm. How? By shifting my thoughts, focusing on good energy, being mindful of what I consume, and using positive affirmations to reinforce my confidence.

Each day I make a conscious choice that, "Today is a good day." If I forget to do this, I find myself in a state of agitation, sweating the small stuff, and just being out of alignment. Using an affirmation like this rewires my thoughts and fears of the day and reminds me that it is MY choice to make it a good day or not.

Just like choosing to have a good day, you have the power to choose what you allow into your life. This makes all the difference when it comes to maintaining a positive energy, and remember the goal is to harness the energy you want to attract into your life.

I choose to be mindful and reject the urge to obsess about my choices, to the best of my ability. This obsession is based in self-doubt and worry, which is not conducive to the process of growth. I do my best to accept the things that are not in my control and choose to take appropriate action for the things that I can control. Having an understanding of the difference between the two is helpful.

Letting go of self-doubt has gifted me the ability to detach from judgment, expectation, and outcome. It took a while but

I've come to the realization that it doesn't matter what other people think. It doesn't matter if the future doesn't look the way I thought it would. I have to be okay with my choices and accept that things don't always go as planned.

Positive self-talk allowed me to eventually free my mind from overthinking and obsessive thoughts. With this clarity, I am able to make decisions, choosing what's best for me, and not what society deems "correct."

Today, I choose what's right for me. No one else can choose for me. If it is not my choice, it will never mean as much. I choose to be happy, joyous and free, because it's my choice to do so.

Affirmation
I breathe in the presence of the moment.
I breathe out the clutter of the mind.
Today is a beautiful day.

Choosing for yourself is empowering as fuck. Let go of any second guessing thoughts. The "should, would, could, what if, what will they think," bullshit only diminishes your power.

Choosing to set boundaries is an amazing way to protect internal energy. You get to choose what you focus on and what you *consume* on a day to day basis. These are the things that you CAN control; your thoughts, your words, what you watch, what you listen to, what you read, the conversations you have, who you vent to, and who you surround yourself with.

Most days I need to consciously make the decision to *choose* to let go. Let go of the small stressors. Let go of the inconveniences of day to day life. Let go of the possible judgement of others.

But that's just the first step.

Let go of the negative thoughts and then embrace the beauty in your world. Connect to gratitude, faith, and the abundance of joy that already exists in your life. This is your choice! You can choose to focus on lack, or you can choose to focus on joy. This is aligning with a higher vibration.

Remember, there is no such thing as "have to" or "supposed to." Those phrases are man made prescriptions that don't actually hold any truth. The way things are, the way things "should be," is based on how you choose to live.

Affirmations help increase self-confidence. Affirmations help support self-belief. Within this space you can achieve clarity, internal peace, and truly know what's right for you. There are unlimited possibilities that are available in this lifetime. Listen to the heart. Feel into the soul. There is no right way or wrong way to live. You get to choose for yourself.

Journal Practice:

1. *How are you at making your own decisions?*
2. *Do you allow outside opinions to persuade your decisions?*
3. *What can you do to be more confident in your choices?*
4. *How can you choose happiness on a day to day basis?*
5. *Create an affirmation to increase your self-confidence in decision making.*

Example: I trust myself and my intuition. I am open to ask for advice, but I am strong in my knowledge to choose for myself.

Chapter 16: Willingness

Affirmation

I am willing to put in the work to achieve my intentions.

I am worthy of living the life of my true desires.

I am able to do hard things.

It is so.

Willing (adjective)

will·ing

> **a:** inclined or favorably disposed in mind : ready
>
> **b:** prompt to act or respond
>
> **c:** done, borne, or accepted by choice or without reluctance

Willingness to take action is another key aspect to this process. This is where you connect to your mental resilience and perseverance. Affirmations are not about saying something will happen and then sitting back and waiting for the miracle to transpire. Yes, you are speaking to the universe and telling it what you want, but then you need to be willing to do whatever it takes to reach your intended goal.

It's like the old saying, "God will move mountains, but you need to bring the shovel." The universe will deliver, but you still need to show up ready to take *solution based action.*

What is solution based action? It is taking tangible steps that are focused on finding a solution. Taking action should be intentional in order to help you reach the top of your mountain. When stepping into a space of action, ask yourself; What *am I willing to do in order to achieve my goals? What can be done right now? Are these steps aligned with the intention?*

Being willing to put words into action is some next level shit. You can say a lot of things, but does the audio match the visual? Are you talking the talk and also walking the walk?

Becoming consistent in your practice of affirmations shows your willingness to take action. With continuous work you will begin to form a habitual routine, which will begin to foster change in your life. Seeing the changes occur can lead to further action because you've started the momentum towards forward movement. The thrill of seeing results, large or small, can be a catalyst to keep going. Be open to willingness. Willingness to work. Willingness to make mistakes. And willingness to stay the course, even when things become difficult.

Willingness is a principle that is pursued by you and only you. No one can force you to be willing to put in the work. No one can force you to make the necessary changes to better yourself. For most, willingness to take action will come when the pain of your awareness becomes great enough. This means that you get to a point where you can't continue the timeline that you're on any longer because of mental or emotional discomfort. This uncomfortable feeling is a blessing because it's usually a push towards major change.

Willingness opens the doors to knowledge, direction, and achievement.
Be willing to know, be willing to do, be willing to create a positive result.
Be willing, especially, to follow your dream.
- Peter McWilliams

In my story, the pain of living in discomfort has often been the motivation for change, specifically when I was 26, 29, and again when I was 33. And okay yes, 34 and maybe even 35.

At 26, I became willing to live a clean lifestyle, free from all mind and mood altering substances. This was not an easy adjustment for me since my main coping mechanism was to escape reality with the use of substances.

At this point in time, I needed to be willing to find new ways to cope with life on life's terms. I absolutely love this saying because the fact is, shit will always happen. Life will eventually throw hard things your way. No matter how perfect your life may seem to be, there will always be challenges to work through. This is why learning healthy ways to cope is extremely important for everyone.

For me, this included attending twelve step meetings regularly, building a support group, beginning an exercise regimen, reading self-help books, and connecting to spiritual practices. Taking on all of these healthy habits helped me to commit to live better, be better, and want better.

It took acceptance, open-mindedness and willingness. I had to become willing to explore new things in order to get past old habits and begin to form new ones. Without willingness, I would have ended up doing the same old things over and over again, and I would have been stuck in the most miserable chapter of my personal story.

At 29, when I made the decision to change my career, I needed to be willing to do the hard work that came along with that shift. I didn't have the luxury of not working while I was in school, or taking my time with the education process. In order to be able to live and also get my degree in a timely manner, I had to be willing to work a full time job, while being a full time student. That was not easy but I needed to continue to be willing to put in the work and do hard things to reach my goal.

This time of my life came with a lot of tears. I was working seven days a week. I was taking four graduate level classes per semester. I took intersession and summer classes, giving myself no breaks in between. And, in the midst of my personal chaos, the world was hit with a deadly pandemic that resulted in my support group meetings to shut down.

I remember thinking that the "go, go, go," would never end. I was constantly overstimulated, overworked, and overwhelmed.

Eventually, I could see the light at the end of the tunnel. I knew what I was working towards and I kept my eye on the end game. After three years of putting one foot in front of the other, I graduated two master programs with a perfect GPA and began my search for a permanent position. I needed to be willing to do whatever it took to continue forward until I got to where I wanted to go. I never gave up and I kept making choices that would set me up for success.

At 33, I was once again faced with a hard choice that asked me to lean into the willingness to take action, the divorce. This moment in time was soul crushing. I remember feeling that a rug was ripped from under me and my whole world was being flipped upside down. There was denial, bargaining, anger, and sadness. All the stages of grief minus acceptance, which would come later.

The truth was I needed to become fully willing to move on and trust my process in order to heal and grow. I had to be willing to make choices to enhance my own future. I needed to become willing to embrace change.

Throughout the entire journey to where I am today, I have always used the practice of affirmations. It has helped me in times of doubt, fear, and paralyzing feelings of hopelessness. Positive self-talk has, and will, continue to enhance my willingness to keep going, because it helps me tune into my sense of worth and self-confidence, no matter what challenges I am facing.

Affirmation
I am aligned with clear intentions.
I am courageously working towards my
dreams & goals.
I am ready & willing to take action.

If you struggle with willingness, affirmations are a beautiful way to help create an openness that is needed to practice this principle. Change of any kind is scary, but you possess the ability within yourself to be resilient and make choices that are going to lead you to the places you want to go; even if there are bumps, twists, turns, and roadblocks along the way.

Staying open-minded and vigilant will continue to help you embrace the willingness to take action and stay the course. Remember, you are powerful and you can do hard things.

Journal prompt:

1. *What are you willing to do for your goals?*
2. *What are you not willing to do?*
3. *What (if anything) is holding you back?*
4. *Create an affirmation to enhance your willingness to move towards your goals.*

Example: I push through discomfort of difficult situations and align myself with the willingness to continue moving forward.

Chapter 17: Gentle Action

Affirmation:

I release the urge to force,
freeing myself to move gracefully.

I step into a state of allowance,
effortlessly connecting to the flow of life.

*I embrace **gentle action**,*
balancing effort, patience & easeful change.

I align with positivity & passion,
truly knowing that no matter the outcome, all is well.

It is so.

Action (noun)

ac·tion

    a: a thing done : deed

    b: the accomplishment of a thing usually over a period of time, in stages, or with the possibility of repetition

    c: actions (plural) : behavior, conduct

Inspired action is making choices and taking steps that are aligned with your desired outcome. They are the steps you take after you have decided what it is you'd like to manifest into your world. It is an essential step because without action, there is no solution.

Inspired action is always solution based. In order to practice inspired action, you must have clear intentions, as well as defined and measurable goals. This means you must know exactly what you want and plan exactly how you intend to get there. Being specific with your affirmations will be the first step, and repeating them each day will affirm to the universe what you want. The second step is the follow through. Take specific intentional actions so you can see your progress throughout the journey.

Goal setting for any aspect of life, whether you want to be magical about it or not, needs to be achievable. While all things in this lifetime are possible, and you can do anything you want to do, sometimes you need to crawl before you can walk. Being realistic and setting a reasonable timeline for yourself will help you stay on track.

I coined the term *gentle action* as a reminder to go easy on myself as I stepped into this new way of being. I've always been great at planning and executing action, but struggled when it came to connecting to the concepts of grace and ease.

Gentle action is all about allowance and release of expectations. Basically, don't force shit! Put in the necessary work and steer your desired outcome by visualizing and verbalizing what you want. Allow the rest to unfold the way it will. If something feels forced, it probably isn't the right action for you, and when you release the attachment, another option will come along that is better suited for your manifestation.

Action and allowance are essential aspects that align your vibration with the universe. Within my journey, forced intentions have always brought me to pain, while easeful allowance has led me to success.

Your belief determines your action
and your action determines your results,
but first you have to believe.
- Mark Victor Hansen

I had this revelation during a trip to New Orleans right after I turned 35. Three months prior, I began to date someone for the first time after my divorce. I was still grieving my marriage and had much healing to do within the notion of partnership. This ultimately took a toll on the newer relationship. The breakup occurred in December, a week before my birthday. There was unforeseen trauma involved in this separation that kicked up a lot of my shit, and I was forced into a state of reflection yet again.

After I entered recovery I found outlets in exercise, spirituality, and travel. So my first thought was to get away. I impulsively planned a trip to Louisiana with my college best friend. It may not have been the best idea since I was in a very depressed state and was heading to one of the biggest party cities in the country; however, it ended up being one of the most surprising spiritual awakenings.

Throughout the time I spent exploring being single, I became hyper-independent. This hyper-independence built a "spiritual armor" that had a negative effect on my mindset. Instead of using spirituality to help me cope and increase faith, it became a defense mechanism that I used to make myself feel safe and protected, in an extremely guarded way.

I was into all forms of spiritual concepts that focused on female power, but was extremely resistant to any male entity, such as God or Jesus. I used my beliefs to feel superior to anyone that followed any type of organized religion. The irony here was that I projected this belief to be innovative and open-minded when in reality, it kept me completely closed off to any other ideologies.

I tell this story because on the trip, my eyes were opened, forcing me into a state of realization. As I explored the city of New Orleans I began to see signs of traditional religions, such as Christianity, which surprised me since my intent was to explore the history of witchcraft and voodoo. Seeking magic brought me to a place where I found the value of God, in all His glory, while simultaneously being enlightened on the Divine Feminine by a Tarot Reader named Ashley.

I used to think the Divine Feminine was about being strong and independent, but the reality is that embracing feminine energy is to accept gentle action and find balance with the divine masculine. I was not doing this. I was embracing masculine energy but disguising it as an independent feminist, thinking this was what divine feminine was all about. I was aggressive in my relationships. I was controlling. I was not graceful and did not handle myself with ease. I began to see the wreckage of this hyper-independence within my relationships and the consequences I endured when I attempted control over people, places, or things. This epiphany was crystal clear.

My closed mindedness and misconceptions were causing a major imbalance. As I began to see this, I started to put the pieces together and found an undeniable pattern of forcing outcomes. The parallels were almost unreal. Going through my history, it was as if I relived the same story again and again.

From my very first boyfriend to the most current situation-ship, there has been a recurring theme of distorted perception, attachment, fear, and force. I was also hyper-centered on the results that I wanted; the kid, the house, and the "life." I wasn't present in the moment within any relationship. I wanted to skip to the "fairy tale ending." I was rushing. I was impatient. I was in a hurry.

One day, as we were venturing down Bourbon Street, we stumbled into a vintage shop after leaving the New Orleans Historic Voodoo Museum on Dumaine Street. I was already in a state of awe at the amount of Jesus and Bible references within a voodoo culture. I was starting to feel some sort of spiritual connection to God, in the traditional sense, which was very unlike me. Coincidences have always been a beautiful sign for me. I embrace them as little winks or indications that I am on the right path. As I was walking through this vintage shop, I looked up and saw this embroidered blanket hanging from the wall that said, *"The hurrier I go, the behinder I get."*

I was stunned. I felt called out by the universe. Up to this point, I felt that I was taking gentle action in all areas of my life, but the truth was, I wasn't. In the area of love, I was anything but gentle and this always produced the same results. Hurt, pain, agony, anxiety, and depression. I was always pushing, trying to accelerate the timeline. Each would end, leaving me in a place where I needed more healing than before.

I felt like a failure. Was my hurried mindset the catalyst to the endless pain that was recurring? The revelation I had at this time gave me the answer. Absolutely, Yes! The missing link was a connection to the concept of gentle action. I was putting in the work but I was forcing all of it. There was no trust, no faith, no easeful energy.

Now, on the opposite end of the spectrum, I could see that when I did embrace gentle action, I was able to be successful. I was thriving in my career and sinking in relationships and I couldn't understand why. Where was the disconnect to manifesting a healthy relationship? It was so obvious now. When it came to building independence in my career, I was always able to let go of attachment to outcome. I would put in the work, but also allow things to unfold naturally. When I'm in that state of allowance, things just seem to happen, without force or control. This is the key. This is the answer. This is the way to manifest.

All of this woke me up to the things I needed to change and the way I navigated action within all areas of my life. I needed to be consistent. I needed to let go of my sense of entitlement to specific results. When I am able to do this I see the light, the positive, and the hope.

So where to begin?

For me, I had to remember the actions I would take when it came to recovery, school, and work.

Step one, speak the words using affirmations.

Step two, take the necessary actions.

Step three, allow it to unfold without expectations or trying to control the exact outcome.

The third step is the faith step. When you trust that the universe will deliver after you say what you want and take the steps needed to make things happen, you are then connected to the frequency of faith and hope, believing that the best possible outcome will occur.

Affirmation

I am aligned with my intentions.
I am taking action to move towards success.
I am trusting the process to unfold in perfect divine timing.

Generally, I don't fuck around. I naturally want to fix problems and get shit done. I will do all it takes to finish what I set out to accomplish. This attitude is helpful but not the end all be all. There are steps to the process and one of the most important steps is to take action but have faith in the universe. Throughout this process, walk with your head high, knowing that you have the power to manifest a life of joy and happiness.

Releasing control and *surrendering* to the unfolding is the practice of allowing all to transpire in the way the universe has intended it to. Do what you can, without expectations, without force, and lean into acceptance of what will come. This is aligning your energy with the universe. This is the most powerful thing you can do. Let go of fear and trust the process.

Journal prompt:

1. *Describe exactly where you are right now and be as specific as possible. Then, describe exactly where you want to be in your desired future.*
2. *What action steps can you take RIGHT NOW to help bring you closer to your goals?*
3. *How can you release attachment and connect to allowance?*
4. *Create an affirmation to connect to the concept of gentle action.*

Example: I see the actions I can take. I am willing to do only what I can. I am open to trusting the process.

Chapter 18: Commitment

Affirmation

*I let go of worried thoughts,
allowing myself to stay present
on the path.*

*I am aligned with what I can control,
understanding that there are
things I cannot.*

*I am regulated within the body & mind,
staying grounded in confidence & hope.*

I am safe. I am focused. I am committed.

It is so.

Commitment (noun)
com·mit·ment

>   **a:** an agreement to do something in the future
>   **b:** something pledged
>   **c:** the state or an instance of being obligated or emotionally impelled

Commitment is essential to creating a life of fulfillment. You need to stay vigilant, take action, and be willing to put in the effort. Staying the course even when things get hard is what separates the creators from the dreamers.

Staying committed takes resilience because things won't always be easy. To be resilient is to have the ability to overcome difficult situations and adapt in challenging times.

"Nothing worth having comes easy," a quote by Theodore Rossevelt, is a phrase that I love because of the sheer and complete honesty behind it. When things come too easy, you don't value it as much. When you have to work for something, it means more to you than anything else. It's like an energetic exchange. The more energy put in, the more sacred it becomes. The journey may be long. The process can be difficult. But over time you will see, as I did, that's the whole point. With hard work and commitment comes personal growth and gratitude for all you've achieved.

The biggest commitment you must keep
is your commitment to yourself.
- Neale Donald Walsch

Recovery was the first time I truly began to value commitment. During my teenage years and early twenties, I very rarely showed up when I said I would. I would constantly miss family events, call in sick to work, and cut classes. I had a mindset of seeing how much I could get away with. How little did I need to do just to simply get by? Because of this, I didn't really value anything. I did not value relationships, school, or my jobs. I didn't care and therefore didn't have any focus or commitment to anything.

Making a decision to get my life back with the help of a twelve step program came with the principle of commitment. First, I committed to attending ninety meetings in ninety days. This concept comes from the idea that it takes ninety days to form a new habit. I started to take on tasks at the meetings to hold myself accountable for showing up. This gave me self-confidence and a sense of responsibility. I began to build relationships within a support group which furthered the concept of commitment, now involving other people and their needs. I also expanded my dedication to my own program by getting involved with step work. This is self-work used to promote the healing of core issues, and identifying why I behaved the way I did for so long.

All of these actions helped me find a value in commitment. Seeing how it was changing my life inspired me to keep up with the forward momentum. I decided to stay *committed* to commitment.

Commitment isn't always easy. It can be draining sometimes. I found that in overwhelming times, it's easier for me to just *show up*. If I show up, I win half the battle. This is the concept of bringing the body and the mind will follow. I use this strategy with the gym all the time. I find if I just get through the front doors, I'm there and usually can begin to rally. The same translated to recovery, to school, and even my career.

It was a huge undertaking when I decided to go back to school. Working full time, paying bills and dealing with a global pandemic, came with a lot of blood, sweat and literal tears. I remember being in the process and thinking that it was never going to get easier. I actually became accustomed to the mentality of; eat, sleep, study, schoolwork, classes, day job, part-time job, gym, repeat. This was my life.

Although I was completely exhausted, I was extremely committed to doing whatever it took to reach my goal. I would take low paying jobs just to build my resume. I took jobs that had horrible commutes, in not so great working environments, all to prove to the universe that I was committed to this manifestation.

I'll say it again, commitment separates the dreamers from the creators. Commitment is the action and willingness to do what it takes to achieve your goals.

While working towards my career goals, I found something intriguing while observing a local Facebook community page for teachers. The page is always flooded with complaining and negative comments about how people cannot find jobs. But in my own experience, I was always able to find a job. I found my first job right out of school. From there, six months later I moved to a second job that was a little more aligned with what I wanted. A year later, I started a full-time probationary position. It was only a year and a half after graduating that I was able to land a stable, secure job.

So, what was the difference? Why was it so seamlessly *easy* for me to find placements and continue to get closer to my goals in such a short period of time, when others were trying six to eight years to find jobs, and giving up in the process?

In my experience, after taking jobs that were mentally and physically taxing, or jobs that didn't come with long term stability, I was able to build my resume and references, which enabled me to land the position I am in today. This was commitment to the process. This was willingness to do the things that needed to be done. This was action.

Not everyone has the fortitude to continue down the path when things get hard. Often I need to remind myself that, "I can do hard things," because I've done hard things before. Most humans have dealt with hardship at least once in their lives, however in the midst of doing hard things, you can forget that you have the ability to get through, just like you always have.

During my time as a student, I recall falling into a space of "I'm not good enough," or "I can't." This is when I had to use affirmations to remind myself that "I can and I will," that I *am* enough. It is helpful when these negative thoughts occur to use a reference point from a time in life when you successfully faced adversity and walked through it to the other side.

For me, my constant reminder of being able to face hard times always comes back to when I got clean and began recovery. When things get tough at any point in my life today, whatever it is I am creating, I remind myself that "I can and I will." I remind myself that I already did the hardest thing of all when I pulled myself out of the grips of addiction and began a new life from nothing.

All of the action, commitment, and positive self-talk led me here, where I get to be a productive member of society, with a career, a home, and relationships with humans that I never would have imagined.

Affirmation
I am focused.
I am determined.
I am committed to the intentions I am manifesting.

I understand that most people think it takes a certain kind of person to be able to pull their lives together, especially when they have fallen so far down. But I don't believe that to be true. I believe every single human being has the power within them to create a life they desire, regardless of their past. The secret is connecting to personal power, having the willingness to take action, and staying committed to that action no matter how hard things get in the process.

Sometimes in this journey one of the hardest concepts to commit to is the dedication to self-love. This is the ultimate commitment to self. I still struggle with this from time to time, which is why I still actively practice affirmations on a daily basis. This is the steadfastness that keeps you going and builds your resiliency. When you fall down, and you will, pick yourself back up. Commitment is not about being perfect. It's about not giving up.

So give yourself a chance. Don't quit before the miracle happens within your own life. If you can see it and feel it, it's yours. Remember to stay the course, trust the process, stay committed, and enjoy the ride.

As you move from this section, focusing on the mind, you will begin to feel into the heart space. You are now moving from your thoughts and actions, and starting to connect into the space of love, trust and faith. Here is where the magic can truly happen.

The connection to the mind and heart will connect you to your inner most powerful self, where you are the creator of any and all things that you wish to bring into form. Let's fucking go.

Journal prompt:

1. *Are you struggling with commitment to yourself and your goals?*
2. *How can you honor your commitments and stay the course of action?*
3. *Create an affirmation to help you stay committed to your process.*

Example: When things get hard, I remember my goals. I am committed to myself and my dreams.

Section Four
"I Love."

The Heart.

Affirmation

I am safe, in this home which is my heart.
I am safe in this place & in this time.

All is well.

The heart space. A concept that sounds so simple but is actually more complex than you would realize. The heart space in general is not an idea that is hard to understand. The complexity comes from grasping the intellection of what it means to absorb the theory into a practice.

So, what is *the* heart space?

Physically, this is the center of your chest, at the area of your actual heart. Energetically, it is the *heart chakra*, which holds the energy of love, acceptance, compassion, and connection.

If you think of the mind as the brain, you can most likely relate to a time when it has become overwhelmed with thoughts. The heart, on the other hand, is not aligned with thoughts but actual feelings and emotions. When you are connecting to the heart, you are leaving behind the habit of overthinking and over analyzing, and allowing yourself to *feel* what it is you want to attract.

Within the next section you will explore your innate ability to tune into the heart space, fully and completely. This takes patience, trust, and faith in the process of your unfolding journey. Surrendering to this process and connecting to self-love will bring you closer to self and closer to the dreams you desire to create in this lifetime.

Chapter 19: Connection

Affirmation

*I am one with the space of my heart,
aligned & connected to my emotions.*

*I am worthy of compassion & kindness,
free from insecurity & doubt.*

*I am innately deserving of an abundance of joy,
finding gratitude in the love that exists within me &
around me.*

It is so.

This chapter is dedicated to my beautiful support group of women. Without you, I wouldn't be where I am today. Thank you for loving me when I didn't feel loveable. Thank you for seeing me through the chaos, tears and hurt of the healing process. Thank you for always showing up. And thank you for reminding me who I am when I felt lost.

Connection (noun)
con·nec·tion

> : the act of connecting : the state of being connected: such as
> **a:** causal or logical relation or sequence
> **b:** relationship in fact
> **c:** a relation of personal intimacy

The mind is all about thought, commitment, planning, and action. The heart is all about emotions. After taking the steps to understand what it is you want, it is time to connect to the *feeling* within your heart. Connecting to the heart space is another aspect of raising your vibration to attract your desired outcome. You visualize it first in the mind, and then feel it in the heart. If you can find that alignment, you are on the right track.

You may be wondering, how do you connect with the heart space? This concept was difficult for me mainly because I tend to live in the mind, overthinking and overanalyzing. A spiritual mentor taught me to simply close my eyes and imagine myself in my brain. After I'd get a clear vision of myself in my mind, I would imagine watching myself move from my mind and into the center of my chest. The only way to connect to the heart is to get out of the mind, and this exercise is a good tool to help settle the thoughts, visualize being in the heart, so you can be in tune with your emotions.

Feel into the heart before the brain muddies it up, is a phrase that came to me in a dream. It says so much and rings so true.

Think about a time when you tapped into your intuition but then moments later second guessed it. This is the brain muddying up the heart space. This is the mind overthinking and blocking the feeling of intuition that is coming from within you. The connection to the heart settles the mind so you can hear and feel what your body is telling you.

The main concept of connection is going to begin with your connection to self. Self-reflection begins with a pause. I will be honest, pausing was never my strong suite. I tend to be a very impulsive person when it comes to acting on my feelings, but this reality has got me into trouble more times than I can actually recall.

The exact nature of this character trait most definitely stems from impatience. It's hard to sit with feelings. I always felt the need to act, or do something, to change the feeling. This is a very common desire for most human beings. The world is a society of wanting things exactly when you want them, and typically these *things* can be obtained quickly and easily. However, when it comes to feeling the feelings, it's not so easy and it's not so quick.

Contemplation is the action of looking within. It is sitting with a thought or feeling and just observing. Not doing anything. Just witnessing and being still to form a deeper understanding of what it actually is. More often than not, this isn't the most comfortable thing to do. Self-reflection, contemplation, and inner connection comes with time, practice, and patience.

Connection with yourself
only comes in moments of silence.
- Bryant McGill

On my journey to connection, I found myself sitting in a church. This may not seem like such a crazy notion, but for me it was out of character. It was New Year's Day of 2025 and

I was in a place of complete hopelessness. I was experiencing an emotional bottom, which I now see as another layer on the journey of self-healing.

Sitting in that pew, on that morning, gave me a sense of calmness that I hadn't experienced in over a month. I felt oddly out of place, yet at home at the exact same time. My usual spiritual practices were journaling, affirmations, and pulling some tarot cards for guidance, but on this day I felt called to be in a place of worship and the church that came to mind, was where my grandmother's funeral was held in 2017.

The ironic part is, for years I had felt extremely uncomfortable in churches. I would joke about my body being set on fire the minute I walked through the door (a witch reference that made me feel *bad* in the best way). On this day, everything was different.

The priest was in the middle of his sermon. I strategically arrived about fifteen minutes late. I sat down, felt a weight lift off my shoulders, and allowed myself to tune in to what was being said.

He spoke about the pause of contemplation. The softness and stillness of self-reflection. This was no coincidence. It was exactly the message I needed to hear at that moment. All this time, eight years to be exact, I always sought healing from outside of myself. I only just began to see this now because I would always disguise my healing modalities as "inner work."

Let me explain.

Exercise was my number one outlet for years. I justified it as a form of meditation, which it can be. However, there is great power and healing within the action of stillness that I yet to truly master.

Journaling and reading were other outlets. Yes, these are inner healing modalities but when I wasn't reading or writing,

I was right back in my head overthinking and obsessing about everything.

Even my spirituality was used as a front. I would say a lot of *things*. Talk a lot of game. I would make spiritual altars, light the candles, go to a lot of yoga classes, meditation sessions, breathwork, you name it. But again, when I wasn't in those spaces of healing, I was back in my head.

Sitting in this church, I saw clearly that I was relying on all of those things to keep me sane, but when those things weren't accessible to me in the present moment, I would be back on my old bullshit.

The missing piece was connection to my inner self. This was the action step I needed to truly embrace. Awareness is great and all. But reflection and awareness without action means nothing will actually change or improve.

The unfortunate reality is that *practicing the pause* is extremely fucking hard. Sitting with yourself, especially when you are going through it, is no joke. I would experience visceral reactions to seeing myself face to face in times of hardship. My anxiety would cause burning sensations within my body that felt like I was about to go up in flames. Holding this discomfort was not ideal, which is why I continued to avoid it for so long.

Being in this church, hearing exactly what I needed to hear, was an *aha* moment. It was something I heard a million times on my journey, but didn't have the ability to truly listen to until this day. The next level of healing would be rooted in the stillness of pause and reflection.

The way I began to incorporate this was to sit in meditation and tune into what I felt physically and emotionally. After time sitting with myself, I turned to my affirmations. Before reading my words out loud, I would imagine what it felt like to feel at peace. I then allowed the physical body to relax and the mind to clear, really embracing the feeling of this serene state. Over time, the stillness became easier and I was soon able to self-regulate using the practice of inner connection.

Connection to self is such an important concept to embrace, but there are more connections to be made on this journey. Connection with others is not something to overlook. I am very grateful for the people in my life today. I have a great family, but I also have an amazing support group that has saved my life on so many occasions.

The women in my life today are so precious to me. In the beginning, I had such a resistance to other women. In recovery, a major suggestion is, *men with the men and women with the women.* During my first year clean, I did not take this suggestion. I was more comfortable hanging around with the guys because they validated me and also didn't make me look at myself.

Around year three, I felt the call to begin connecting with women. This was transformational. These connections helped me to grow in ways I never knew I could. They would call me on my bullshit, in the most gentle and kind ways. They would let me cry and complain until I released whatever it was that was holding me in dark places. They helped me learn compassion and forgiveness, which ultimately created space for healing in other relationships. And, most importantly, they would show up for me and become a force of presence in my life that made me feel loved and cared for.

Affirmation
I am lovable.
I am loved.
I am love.

Connecting to self is something everyone has the ability to do. Becoming more intuitive lies in trusting and knowing oneself.

Being stuck in the mind blocks this connection. Being stuck in the mind is the biggest defect of the human experience.

I believe that one of the aspects of the soul's journey is to release the control of the mind, and step into feeling from within the heart. With the help of affirmations, self-reflection, and connection with like minded people, the *practice of pause* can help you to clear the mind, align with the heart, and cultivate your desired reality.

Journal prompt:

1. *What makes you feel the most connected?*
2. *How can you strive to stay in that connection on a daily basis?*
3. *Create an affirmation to help you connect to your heart.*

Example: I release the control of the mind. I fall into the space of my heart.

Chapter 20: Faith & Trust

Affirmation

I am calm,
having trust in myself, the universe
& my path.

I am peace,
having acceptance in each moment, experience & life
lesson.

I am serene,
having faith that all is well, beautiful
& joyful.

Being within the presence of this moment,
It is so.

Faith (noun)

> **a:** firm belief in something for which there is no proof : complete trust
> **b:** something that is believed especially with strong conviction

Faith and trust are the principles that allow you to walk through your fears and step into your personal strength. It's in this state where you can fully manifest your intentions because you are connected to your inner power; believing that you are guided, protected, and trusting the process of the unknown.

Fear is the exact opposite of faith. Fear is anxiety, worry, and mistrust that things will not work out for the best. Fear is resistance to the unknown. Fear holds you back from growth because it tends to keep you stuck in your comfort zone, even if the places you are "comfortable" in, aren't necessarily good for you and your future. Fear can be paralyzing for some people. But fear is also an illusion.

Fear develops when you get fixated on all the possible negative outcomes to a situation. This leads to anxiety. Fear and anxiety are formed in your mind. It is an illusion of what can possibly occur. When your own thoughts are running the show, it makes you worry about things that may or may not actually happen.

Rational fears do exist. These are fears based on self-preservation. These instincts arise when you get hurt, threatened, or if you are sensing a bad vibe about someone, or something. These fears are healthy forms of protection. I'm not talking about healthy fears.

I'm talking about fears that hold you back from trying new things; like a fear of change, or fear of failure that results in not even trying. Those are the imaginary fears that you want to get rid of. And how do you get rid of them? You free yourself of fear by allowing yourself to connect to faith. When you connect to faith, you can feel safe within yourself.

Fear based decisions are choices that you make to "preserve" your well being. These anxieties are usually formed by past experiences of similar situations. This is the "what if" mentality. *What if I fail? What if I get rejected? What if they judge me?* In contrast to these negative questions, *what if something amazing happens?* That is a faith based thought.

Faith based decisions are the exact opposite to fear based, where you can make decisions fully trusting that all will work out, even if it doesn't work out as planned. This is the belief that all experiences are necessary, regardless of the outcome. For example, if you try something new or put yourself out there in a different or challenging scenario, but you end up *failing*, it isn't really a failure. You got to experience the new situation and also learn a lesson that you can take with you.

Fear is at the core of a lot of decision making. Even for the people who do a lot of work on themselves. Even for people who appear confident. This is natural within the human experience because the mind is so complex. I tend to fool myself into fearful narratives, such as "I'm not good enough," or "that could never work," or "I don't deserve that."

As I was contemplating the difference between fear and faith when it comes to decision making, I realized that this is a duality that exists. *Duality is two truths existing simultaneously.* It is okay to be both fearful and faithful. It's ok to feel more than one emotion at the same time. The key is to feel that fear and find a way to take action, in spite of it.

Faith is unseen but felt,
faith is strength when we feel we have none,
faith is hope when all seems lost.
- Catherine Pulsifer

One specific area of my life where I tend to be more fear based is within relationships. Whether these are friendships, meeting new people, or within romantic partnerships, my worries always stem from fear of rejection and abandonment. Side effects of this fear have kept me from opening up to new people and new experiences. Talking about duality, it's kind of ironic. Those who know me will say that I am very outgoing and talkative. But when put into a situation where I do not know everyone, I tend to become closed off and quiet.

On the flipside, I am faithful in my decisions in the area of my career and creative abilities. This is exactly why I have been able to become successful when manifesting my goals in teaching and also creating this book. I have a lot of confidence in this practice when it comes to manifesting my own ambition, but I tend to fall short when stepping into confidence within relationships. Because of this, I was actually very fearful of even writing this book. I feared judgment from people who know that I struggle. I felt that they would assume I was a fake and phony when talking about things like faith and trust.

This is where my personal affirmation practices continue to be useful in my life. I had to remind myself that I am still doing the work. I can help others by sharing this practice because it has helped me, and continues to help me to grow into my power. This work has shown me there can be both. You can fear the unknown in some areas of your life, while being extremely open and faithful in others. This is my experience.

"Everything has a way of working itself out," a beautiful quote gifted to me by an Uber driver in Louisiana at the end of

2024. This is a statement of trust. This is a statement of faith. You need both faith and trust to truly believe a statement like this.

I heard these words exactly when I needed it. I was in the middle of an existential crisis and was struggling with my self-worth and confidence.

I was on another level of my healing journey and was beginning to feel a strong urge to re-establish my relationship with spirituality, a.k.a. my faith. I was yearning to find the purest form of faith. True trust in the universe, without pride, without ego. I was starting to see that up to this point, my spiritual practices turned into a defense mechanism, to help me cope with the multiple failed relationships I was continuing to experience. The questions I asked myself were; *How do I let go of fear? How can I be less defensive and closed off, and become more trusting?*

I mentioned in an earlier chapter about action, the concept of spiritual armor. Real spiritual armor is to have full trust and faith that God, or any higher power, will grant you strength and protection. However, my spiritual armor had nothing to do with trust in my spiritual faith. My armor was keeping me on a high horse of self-protection, which made me judgemental and closed off.

Why is this important to explain? Because at one point I did have faith and trust that helped me feel connected and safe to manifest. However, along the way my life experiences, specifically my divorce, tested my faith, trust was lost, and I became resentful and bitter.

With this awareness, I knew I had to rebuild. I was stuck in repeated patterns, which was dimming my ability to manifest the things I wanted for my life. I had to become more open to faith and let go of my fear to come to a space of gentle, graceful ease.

The action I decided to take was to practice the feeling of what calmness actually felt like. My life felt so chaotic and I wanted to rid myself of fear based thinking and resentment. I wanted to be open. I wanted to feel safe within myself. I wanted to feel connected to the energy of real peace and love.

The practice was simple, but also difficult to maintain. I sought out places that helped me identify the feeling of calmness, but I couldn't rely on having to go outside of myself to find this feeling of serenity. I had to go within. I would close my eyes and connect to a feeling of peace.

What did peace feel like in my body? What did peace feel like in my mind? What did peace feel like in my heart?

In my body this felt like relaxation. In my mind it felt like clear and loving thoughts. And in my heart it felt like lightness, like the weight of anxiety was being lifted. I had to practice this often. In the beginning, I would find peace in the moment but the same anxious, fearful feelings soon followed. Eventually over time, this visualization technique allowed me to find peace within myself by letting go and trusting that everything was okay in the moment.

To continue this renewed exploration, I had to re-establish my self-worth with the use of affirmations. I started to create affirmations that focused on faith and trust in God. Yes, the traditional depiction of God. I felt this connection would help lift the resistance I was experiencing and increase my sense of hope. These affirmations definitely felt more prayer-like than anything I had ever done before. But as I mentioned earlier, prayer and affirmations are the same.

The positive self-talk I used helped me build hope. I spoke words to release fear and obsessive thoughts, and I asked for increased faith so that I may connect to peace. My words began to help me trust that all was unfolding perfectly in divine timing. It encouraged me to walk with courage and patience. My new found faith brought about a feeling of grace and ease, and blanketed me in the comfort of unwavering belief.

Affirmation
I am connected to the feeling of peace.
I am connected to the state of calm.
I am connected to the space of ease & grace.
I have faith that all is well.

Sometimes I still make fear based decisions, but there are also many times I am making bold as fuck decisions. Like deciding to become an author, or opening my mind to a deeper relationship with spirituality.

Fear and faith are allowed to exist at the same time. This is the duality of life. The light and the dark. The yin and the yang. Connection to these contrasting energies enables you to grow while acknowledging the things that may need work, and also praising yourself for the things that you're kicking ass at.

The quote, "Faith and fear both demand you to believe in something you cannot see. You choose," by author Bob Proctor, is a good reminder that you have a choice to shift your thoughts from negative to positive, or from fear to faith. Keep doing the work, keep connecting to affirmations, and eventually that faith will flow over into all areas of your life, outshining the fear and allowing you to step into a place of power and progress.

Journal prompt:

1. In what areas of your life do you make fear based decisions?
2. What areas in your life do you make faith based decisions?
3. *Create an affirmation to release your fear and connect with the energy of faith.*

Example: I let go of my fears of the unknown and welcome the endless possibilities that potentially exist.

Chapter 21: Surrender

Affirmation

I surrender my obsession with the past
& the future.

I forgive myself for mis-takes
& repeated patterns.

I connect to happiness & joy
in the here & now.

It is so.

Surrender (verb)

sur·ren·der

> **a:** to yield to power or control
> **b:** to give oneself up into the power of another
> **c:** to give oneself over to something (such as an influence)

The term surrender may sound like *giving up* or *quitting*, however, it's the polar opposite when it comes to spiritual practices.

Surrender is the release of control. It is the practice of allowance. It is the ability to align with acceptance in order to fully let go of attachment to the past, and the possible outcomes of the future.

Acceptance is understanding and patience with all that exists within the present moment. It's the ability to see things as they are in your current reality, without judgment and without obsession. Obsessive thoughts are the illusion of control. The idea that if you overthink, or over analyze a situation, you can somehow change the outcome.

When you allow yourself to fully surrender to the process, you officially let go of specific outcomes. This opens the door for more possibilities to occur, maybe even possibilities you didn't even think of, or didn't know you wanted. Attachment to an outcome keeps your focus on one door and one door only. The space of surrender gives you the opportunity to see all potential doors, and windows, that exist in your life.

It seems like such a simple concept, but the act of surrender can be difficult. People try to control outcomes because it limits the one thing that scares humans the most, the unknown. Surrender means to let go of *control of* what *could* happen. Control, or the illusion of it, limits manifestation powers by blocking potential scenarios. In a world of endless possibilities, the last thing you want to do is stifle yourself by blocking opportunities with your own mental fixation, blinding yourself from the bigger picture.

Try something different – surrender.
- Rumi

The perfect story for surrender is my obsession with the past and future. My obsessive thoughts provide a false sense of control, which messes up my ability to enjoy the present moment. I was never happy because I was too focused on my intended outcome, and the mistakes I made along the way. I couldn't detach from the past. And because of this, I anxiously over-thought the future and how I wanted it to look.

I clearly remember early January of 2025. I was in my head replaying every second of the last few days of my most recent dating experience, over and over again. It was nothing but insanity. The obsession was focused on regret, guilt and shame of my recurring patterns that were pulling me further and further away from my desired life.

I do this often, constantly thinking about the past and how I "should" have done better. No matter how much I think about what has already happened, it will not change the fact that it did. It's done. It's gone. It's unchangeable. The past is the past. There is no going back. There is no rewrite of the script. It already is. There's no point in reliving it, wishing I made different (or better) choices. Surrendering to what has already occurred is the only way to move forward and heal from the pain.

I also do this with the future. I can easily obsess over what will be and try to manipulate everything in order to get there. This has always been my fast track into a state of depression and regret. The way I would try to control outcomes continually landed me in a space of loss. I was never satisfied. I always wanted more. I always had high expectations of other people. I needed to surrender my fixation on the past and future, and learn how to forgive myself for allowing them to have power over my present.

An old friend of mine once said to me, "I just want to be happy."

When he said it, I didn't really hear him. I was blocked because I didn't even know what it meant to just be happy within my current reality. I was always working towards a specific vision, or a project of some kind, and I would miss out because I was too busy looking at the finish line. I was blind to the experience of joy in the moment. I needed to begin appreciating the present moment, with the present people and the present experiences, without feeling the need to force a hypothetical ending. This is surrender.

Affirmations help me to surrender. It all goes back to cultivating trust and faith. I just wanted happiness, whatever that looked like. I wanted hope that all would be well. I wanted to shake the urge to fixate on what had already happened and what might be later on. Surrendering to happiness brought me to a place of understanding that what's meant for me will always find me, and it will be uniquely perfect for me.

I wrote and spoke words of faith and courage. I began practicing mirror work to help me find confidence in the present moment. I have always been prone to depression and anxiety so being present came with a lot of discomfort. Mirror work was something I avoided. But in the moment of complete desperation to be healed of my obsession, I finally took the suggestion. I would take my affirmations of surrender and faith, and speak them as I looked at myself in the mirror. This practice helped me feel comfortable in my own skin, which ultimately gave me strength and hope in the presence of now.

Let's look at an experience that proves surrender does actually work!

When I was working as a part-time teacher, without long-term security, I absolutely loved my job and was very focused on earning a full-time position for the following school year. In February of 2023, it looked like that was exactly what was going to happen when I got a verbal offer for a permanent job after a teacher put in for retirement. Needless to say I was ecstatic and right away stopped my job search. Relief set in. I felt that I actually manifested my dream job.

About a month later, rumors started to circulate that the school was making budget cuts. The word was that the retirement position I was supposed to be taking over was going to be absorbed, instead of filled. This caused a lot of anxiety. I gave up potential interviews and demo lessons because I was banking on this position being mine (side note for all the future teachers out there, never do that unless you have SIGNED an official contract).

When the rumors ended up being true I became overwhelmed with the "poor me" mentality. I couldn't understand why it didn't work, and why I wasn't able to finally complete the manifestation that I was working towards for almost two years. I probably wallowed for a day or two, which sometimes is part of the process as well, and then I remembered that I needed to surrender and trust the process.

I got back to work. I started by creating a new affirmation, specifically focused on *any* outcome that would be best for me. I took action by applying to jobs, speaking to my direct supervisor about being a reference, and went on every single interview that I was offered. Even if I didn't think I wanted to work at a specific school, I showed up anyway. This was me showing the universe that I was serious and I was going to reach my goal before the upcoming school year. I ended up getting eleven interviews, six demo lessons, and two job offers which was highly unusual. I was so extremely blessed with an enormous amount of opportunities, and I ended up landing the perfect job for me.

The most important part of this story was my willingness to take action, my surrender to specific outcomes, and my full trust and faith in the process.

When I surrender, I welcome what is truly meant for me and trust the universe will guide me to my highest potential. I'm grateful for the opportunities and the learning experiences that occurred on my journey, even the ones that have caused pain. In those moments, the practice of surrender brought me to new levels of growth. Having faith that I am where I am supposed to be, and that my path will unfold accordingly, has allowed me to truly let go and live my life in the present moment.

My experiences helped me become more connected to the idea of surrendering. When I fixate on something, I cannot see the whole picture. When I allow all possibilities into my world, I open myself up to aligning with the perfect outcome for me. In times of doubt, positive self-talk has continuously increased my confidence and belief in the journey.

Affirmation
I surrender to the presence of this moment.
I am taking in the beauty of the here and now.
I am at peace with all that is.

Remember, surrender won't always be easy. Faith and trust will help this process. Holding onto specific outcomes will limit the endless possibilities that exist in your world. *You can't grab new opportunities when your hands are full of stuff*, like the past and future. Open your mind and eyes to unlimited experiences in the presence of this moment. Allow yourself to let go. Let things unfold naturally, without force and without attempting control.

Journal prompt:

1. *What does surrender mean to you?*
2. *Are you comfortable with this practice?*
3. *How can you fully surrender and trust that all will work out the way it's supposed to?*
4. *Create an affirmation to help you let go of false control and connect with faith and trust. Speak it to yourself in the mirror every morning and night.*

Example: I let go of the illusion of control. I surrender to trust in my journey.

Chapter 22: Self–Love

"

Affirmation

I release fear.
I release insecurity.
I release second guessing myself.

I call in faith.
I call in confidence.
I call in love & trust in myself.

I connect to peace.
I connect to forgiveness.
I connect compassion for myself.

It is so.

"

Compassion (noun)

com·pas·sion

: sympathetic consciousness of others' distress together with a desire to alleviate it

Love is the most powerful energy that exists. It has been said that love can heal all things. When you view *love* as a frequency of energy, it makes perfect sense to why it is known as a healing vibration. When you share love, or feel loved, you are connected to a higher frequency. It's arguably the best feeling humans have access to. Love gives a sense of belonging, which is major when it comes to human emotional survival.

Abraham Maslow, an American psychologist, composed a theory focused on the human *hierarchy of needs*. Within these needs, love and belonging plays an essential role. Without it, people cannot truly find their purpose.

The theory explains the basic needs that any human has in order to connect to their true selves and true purpose. His model is laid out in the shape of a pyramid. The base of this pyramid is all about basic survival needs such as air, water, food, and sleep. The next level is essential to surviving in this dimension and is based on security and safety, i.e. career, income, home, clothing, health, and resources.

As you move up the pyramid, you arrive at love and belonging. Here lies the importance of human connection, community, and relationships. Without this level being present in a person's life they cannot continue the process of self-actualization, where you achieve purpose and meaning.

If we dissect the pyramid it's clear to see that without love and belonging, humans cannot find that connection to self, which is why this is the most powerful energy that exists.

But here's a major secret that people don't always talk about. Love and belonging can also come from within you. Although human connection is necessary for your overall well-being, you can also cultivate love for yourself by tapping into your own personal power. Once you can love yourself, not only can you elevate your vibration, but you can also love others on a much deeper level.

How can you begin to connect to this type of love? Firstly, be kind to yourself. Use loving words when speaking to, or about, yourself. Keep a positive mindset around who you are and what you do. And give yourself grace when reflecting on the past, present, and future.

Finding the connection to self-love begins with self-compassion. Self-compassion is self-love. A major aspect of this practice is forgiveness. Everyone has regrets, everyone has made mistakes. Loving yourself is showing compassion. Loving yourself is forgiving your past. Loving yourself moves you forward towards your envisioned future.

Peace comes from within.
Do not seek it without.
- Buddha

I can be very hard on myself. I hold myself to high expectations and standards and when I don't meet them, which happens often since I'm human, I beat myself up or compare myself to others. This often leads to resentments, which is an ugly and completely toxic energy.

Somewhere in my upbringing I picked up the habit of perfectionism. Was this character trait developed by gymnastics, where I was constantly criticized and judged by super intense adults? Or was this developed as a coping mechanism as a result of not feeling good enough during my childhood years? I do feel that untangling past trauma is extremely helpful in personal growth, but sometimes awareness of an internal issue is enough to make a change, with or without identifying the exact origin of the behavior. As discussed, having awareness is a catalyst for change. In my case, I needed to let go of high expectations and self-judgment, and begin to practice empathy for myself.

I always have to remind myself that it's okay to not be perfect. It's part of the human experience. It is a true belief of mine that compassion and patience for self is vital for any healing journey. I love the saying, *put down the bat and pick up a feather.* I first heard this in 2016, when I entered recovery, and it has stuck with me throughout my journey, because it is so relevant in my own life. Part of my process has been, and sometimes still is, all about loving myself exactly as I am in this moment. When you can find the connection to being content and whole as you are, you can then truly love yourself. This is a major step on the path to self-validation.

The practice of self-love is being able to stand in your power to make healthy decisions, even when they are extremely hard and cause emotional pain. Self-love is about choosing you, and putting your needs first, in order to live a life that is best aligned for you. Remember, be patient throughout the process.

My ultimate expression of self-love was when I chose to let go of the relationship I had with my ex-husband. After the divorce, we continued a friendship that eventually led to us being together again in a type of companionship. This was a decision based on fear and codependent tendencies. We played the game of our situationship for about three months, during the summer of 2024, until one day the pain started to become great enough for me to begin to really look at the big picture.

It wasn't an easy choice. It was something I deeply struggled with. But I needed to accept the misalignments within the relationship. I needed to put myself first. I needed to show myself love. This didn't mean a lack of love for him as a person, but an abundance of love for me. I needed to walk through my shadow and fears of being alone and starting over at 34. I needed to have faith that this choice would open up new doors and lead to the future that I had always envisioned.

Months after that decision, when I was still struggling with truly embracing self-love, I found myself in Jackson Square in New Orleans. I had just left the famous St. Louis Cathedral and was feeling a real sense of peace and love that I hadn't felt in a while.

I decided to take myself out on a first date. I heard the concept of "dating yourself" many times but never actually tried it. I took a walk in the square, found a bench and just sat. I enjoyed the surroundings, the sun on my face, and the people walking around with their loved ones.

I closed my eyes and began to just feel into the feeling of love that was flowing around me in that moment. As my eyes were closed I heard music in the background that caught my full attention almost immediately.

I got up and started walking towards the sound. It was a song I'd never heard before and it was being sung so beautifully that I just had to go see. As I approached the scene, there was a man with his small little dog, belting out this song that hit my heart. It was *Change Will Come* by Sam Cooke.

There been times that I thought
I couldn't last for long
But now, I think I'm able

To carry on
It's been a long
A long time coming, but I know
A change gon' come
Oh yes, it will

This song, in this second, felt like one of those God moments. I felt like I was being shown things purposely to propel me forward into the next chapter of my life. I sat on the sidewalk, right there in the middle of New Orleans, and just listened to this man sing. I felt so at peace. I felt filled with love. I felt safe within myself.

I stayed there for sometime, tipped the man a few dollars, and continued my date with myself. I started to walk the perimeter of the square, admiring all the artwork being sold. I thought to myself how beautiful the world was and honored that this beauty always exists as long as I am present to really experience it.

After buying a small piece of art, an abstract drawing of a map of the square, which I couldn't resist as a souvenir to commemorate the day, I sat on the grass inside the walls of Jackson Square. I noticed some flowers off in the distance. As I stared at them it was all so clear. I was beautiful as I was. I didn't need outside things to show me love in order to feel worthy. I was loved, not only by my family and friends, but also by myself. I took out my phone and wrote a short letter to myself;

Affirmation
Dear beautiful flower,
No one needs to come around & pick you,
because you are rooted within yourself.

So, how do you practice self-love? Allow yourself to feel. Feel your feelings, without judgment. Allow yourself to be sad, to cry, to scream. But, as a friend of mine once said, "Wipe the tears, don't live in them." This means allow yourself to heal and feel, but don't let it consume you. The love you desire comes from within you.

Acceptance and surrender combined, is in essence, the act of self-love. You accept yourself for who you are and begin to honor the path you are on. Then you surrender to the present moment, fully believing that all is well, exactly as it is, in this space and time. This is loving yourself as a human being but also loving your life experiences, regardless of the different facets of the journey. Self-love is accepting and loving the *good* and the *bad*. And while defining "good" and "bad" can be subjective, accepting both within you, as you interpret all your experiences, is true love for self.

Journal prompts:

1. *Make a list of qualities that you love about yourself. This can be physical, mental, emotional or spiritual. Read the list (outloud or in your head) and finish the list with the statement, "I love you." To enhance this, practice in front of a mirror.*
2. *Create an affirmation to enhance your own self-love.*

Example: I am loveable. I am loved. I am love.

Chapter 23: Patience

"

Affirmation

I open my heart to the peace of patience.

*I open my mind to the calmness
of contentment.*

I open myself to the tranquility of trust.

It is so.

"

*Dedicated to my grandmother,
Carmela Santomauro*

Patient (adjective)

pa·tient

    a: bearing pains or trials calmly or without complaint
    b: steadfast despite opposition, difficulty, or adversity

Let's take it back now to my childhood. All my life I've had a hard time with the word *patience*. I've always been in a rush and always wanting things to happen immediately, if not sooner. Waiting was not my strong suit. I had a deep committed affair with instant gratification, which is why I was so prone to addictive behaviors and things that made me feel good in the moment. The problem with this? I couldn't sustain this "good" feeling for long periods of time.

Instant gratification is acting out on behaviors or making decisions that sacrifice long-term benefits in order to achieve a less rewarding outcome that has an immediate effect. The issue is that these immediate benefits usually act as bandaids of fulfillment and end up hurting you in the long run. Especially when it's keeping you from your overall desires.

My relationship with patience has been a long, bumpy road, filled with discomfort, a lot of pain, and a lot of tears.

My grandmother, Carmela, would always say to me, "Patience my dear."

And I never failed to respond with, "I don't have any."

I have a clear memory of when this interaction first began. I must have been a freshman in high school. My grandmother, whom we called Nanny, knew me well. I was always waiting for the next phase of life, thinking "I'll be happy when..."

Nanny on the other hand was the exact opposite. She was so patient, kind, compassionate, and present. She always showed up for others with a smile on her face. Her patience for me back then was undeniable. I was always getting into trouble and always needed her to bail me out, literally and figuratively. She kept my secrets. She listened to me cry and complain. She was everything to me. Without her influence, I don't know if I would be the same today.

The way she carried herself inspired me. She had an energy about her that I still strive to obtain. It doesn't come to me easily though, which often makes me feel disappointed. It seemed so effortless for her. But then again, I didn't walk in her shoes, so I can't make that assumption.

Let's go back to me never being satisfied in the moment. I couldn't find the patience to just be and enjoy the ride. It was a constant struggle, not only in my teenage years but well into my adult life. The lack of getting to where I wanted to be in my own time frame made me extremely frustrated.

Frustration is an easy way to fall into a space of hate, the exact opposite of love. To release the feeling of tense frustration, you must embrace patience. Frustration distorts the energy flow within your body and mind. The energy that flows within you is your source of power. Aligning yourself with a patient mindset can help you remain in the frequency of love.

You can use affirmations, breathing techniques, or meditation as practices to help you remain patient. It's in the frequency of peace and calmness, growing from the principle of patience, that allows the energy within your life to flow smoothly. Ultimately aligning your heart and mind to the vibrations in which you can create a joyful, peaceful reality.

Patience is the calm acceptance
that things can happen in a different order
than the one you have in mind.
- David G. Allen

Lack of patience is the lack of acceptance of the present moment, thinking it would be better *if* this. I'll be happy *when* that. Or the grass is greener over there.

Remember, serenity equals acceptance and acceptance equals patience.

I got divorced at the age of 33. It was a hard reality to accept. Starting over in my thirties? Terrifying! My impatient attitude was based on perceived norms (fucking society!). My fixation with what my future *should* look like created tense energy. It took almost two years to fully be in a state of contentment with myself.

It came after a point of healing. One of those soul crushing experiences that life just needed to throw at me.

After the divorce I spent a lot of time floating in the wind not knowing if I believed in anything anymore. It was one of those hopeless states that I didn't even realize I was in. I spent so much time trying to rush into the next phase of my life. I didn't want to be where I was and the worst part, I was in complete denial about it.

It took divine intervention to bring me to a state of awareness. There was major work that needed to be done. My energy was off and I desperately wanted to come back to myself.

The truth is, some things take time. For me it took the act of letting go. Trying to control everything around me was not helping. It was just causing more resistance within me, blocking my energy and getting in the way of the joyful, peaceful future I so desired.

I came back to my practices. I started to reconnect to my spiritual beliefs by practicing meditation and using my daily affirmation as a continuous mantra whenever I felt my mind straying.

I did this religiously for three months straight. At first, nothing really changed. Eventually, my mood seemed to get a little lighter. Shifts began to occur and everything seemed to be getting easier. And then one day in February 2025, everything felt different.

It was a day like any other. I woke up, began my morning routine, and then I noticed it. The hurt and frustration of the last few months (really years) was all of a sudden gone.

It was the first time in a long time that I felt truly content; no shame, no regret, no anger, no sadness. It was a miracle. I wasn't internally kicking and screaming, wishing my life was different or obsessing about past "mistakes." I was grateful and felt blessed to have time for me to grow, heal, and write. I was truly in a space of acceptance; embracing patience for myself, patience for my current life, and patience for the thing I want in the future.

This was a direct result of the teachings here in this book. This manifestation took some time but eventually I got it. I manifested acceptance. I manifested patience. How? By connecting to hope.

Here is a secret that I need to tell you; **healing takes patience.**

Once I could accept the past, I could comprehend that I was powerless over what had happened because it already happened. With this came acceptance of the present moment, and patience for myself for exactly where I was. This acceptance was the freedom to peace within myself, right here in the presence of now.

Time and self-healing allowed me to see this. Once I achieved clarity, I was able to make a choice to let go of control and be in the energy of gratitude and faith. No need to rush. No need to force.

Remember, *"The hurrier I go, the behinder I get."* Every situation I have pushed in my life has landed me back at the beginning, or sometimes even further behind then I started. Patience and gentle action are very similar concepts. Both calling for the need to slow down, allow things to unfold without force, and surrender to the universe. With all the forcing and rushing I have done in my lifetime, it was painfully obvious, I needed to be more patient.

Identifying this pattern was an epic shift for me. It was evident that my *rushed* mentality was blocking my peace. Affirmations helped to calm my mind and settle into the trust that everything would be okay, even if it wasn't on my timeline.

Affirmation
I am calm.
I am peace.
I am serene
Being within the presence of this moment.

Sometimes it feels like you're waiting forever to be healed or to turn the page into the next chapter of your life. I often remind myself that nothing worth having comes easy. Sometimes you need to take more time in order to get to exactly where you need to be, and that's okay. There is hope for those who just hold on and learn to be fucking patient.

You are responsible for your peace. This is accepting your current reality, having the patience to do the work, wait for the future, and having joy and gratitude in the here and now.

Holding space for yourself while you are waiting can be difficult, but you can do hard things, even if it hurts. Patience is key.

Mahatma Gandhi said, "To lose patience is to lose the battle."

Anytime you lose your patience you immediately begin to rush, or force, outcomes. This usually results in resistance that causes great setbacks, pain, or regret. Continuously connecting to the energy you want to attract will help you to stay in a state of peace, calmness, and surrender. When you are at peace with your current reality, trusting that all will work out, you can have the patience to move at the pace of the universe. Sometimes it may be fast, and at other times it may be slow and steady. No matter what, tuning into patience will always ensure that you are projecting the energy of ease and grace.

Use your affirmations to let go of resistance and find the courage to walk through fear, pain, and uncertainty. Use your affirmations to build confidence in yourself to embrace the unknown. And of course, practice patience, keep your faith, and trust that what is meant for you *is* yours. Even if you need to wait a little longer for it to arrive.

Journal prompts:

1. *Where are you lacking patience today?*
2. *How can you instill the practice of patience and tolerance to those areas of your life?*
3. *How can you use patience to attract the energy you want in your life?*
4. *Create an affirmation to promote patiences in your life.*

Example: I clear the urge to force or rush. I am in tune with the energy of peace, calm, & patience. All is well.

Chapter 24: Gratitude

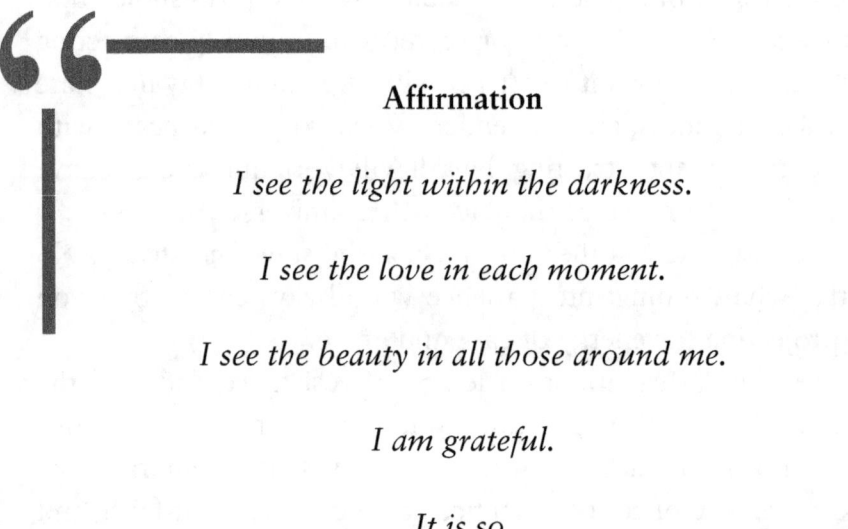

Affirmation

I see the light within the darkness.

I see the love in each moment.

I see the beauty in all those around me.

I am grateful.

It is so.

Grateful (adjective)
grate·ful

> **a:** appreciative of benefits received
> **b:** expressing gratitude
> **c:** affording pleasure or contentment : pleasing

To have real power behind your words is to unite with positive energy. Positive energy comes from a positive outlook on life, which comes from the practice of gratitude. Yes, gratitude! I'm sure many are familiar with this word, and may even have a consistent practice. It's almost impossible to speak about self-affirmation, and the power of words, without mentioning it.

For those who are new on your journey, gratitude is the practice of focusing on all the wonderful things you have in your current life. In essence, gratitude is the act of being thankful. This can be focusing on the people in your life, a job, any material things, and it can also be showing appreciation for the little things we tend to take for granted; running water, heat, shelter, clothing, food, etc. The magic behind gratitude is being intentional about how you focus your mind and energy.

Positive energy and gratitude go hand in hand. One cannot exist without the other.

Reminder, the purpose of affirmations is to connect with your voice, a.k.a. your personal vibration. The connection to your vibration raises your frequency and in turn attracts positive energy. This is the concept you have already been practicing to meet the vibration of the universe.

Gratitude helps to increase your vibration by allowing you to be present in the positive outlooks of life. This is seeing the good within the bad, being happy and thankful for everything you have, even if you feel that you want more. It's knowing and trusting that you have everything you need and all that you want will come to you at the perfect, divine, time. This is the practice of faith, presence, and surrender.

When I first got my life in order, adopting the practice of gratitude wasn't an easy process. I am a natural complainer. I used to complain often, sometimes without any awareness of even doing it. Still today I will have my moments, but I use my tools to identify the behavior, change it, and bring myself into a state of gratitude. Some days are easier than others. Complaining has been a lifelong habit for me. Being mindful of this tendency was a serious shift because it helped to reroute my thoughts and experience the positive, instead of defaulting to the negative.

The way I stay connected on a daily basis is starting my day with a gratitude list. This helps me become grounded, honoring all the things I have in my life, and allows me to connect to the concept of *presence*.

Presence is the act of being present, *existing in the now*, and simply being in the moment. I love the saying, "Keep your head where your feet are." Your feet can only be in one place, and that is the exact moment you are in. On the contrary, although your physical body is in the exact moment, your mind can stray from present to past to future, back to the past, into a fantasy, all within a split second. The concept of keeping your head where your feet are, is the practice of bringing your mind into the present, not allowing it to wander off into a space of worry, anxiety or depression.

The Language of Self-Affirmation

In order to cultivate a positive attitude,
we must first cultivate a sense of gratitude.
- Dalai Lama

Gratitude has been an ongoing, but also fleeting, practice for me throughout the years. I write a gratitude list each day but that does not mean every day is one where I feel grateful. I think this is a normal human experience. The ebbs and flows of feeling good and then feeling down. I can be hard on myself about it, thinking I am doing it wrong. But I try to stay in a place of self-compassion, reminding myself that I can't be perfect all the damn time.

Closing out the year in 2024, I was in a place of depression and regret. I was not connected to gratitude or positive thinking which fueled the hopelessness even more. I was disappointed. I just turned 35 and I wasn't where I *thought* I would be. I was divorced and single. These two facts were my entire focus during December and into the beginning of 2025.

The hyperfocus I had on the things that didn't work out was once again robbing me of joy and keeping me from being present. I am beyond thankful for the people in my life. I have an abundance of beautiful support ranging from family, friends, and friends who are family. Without these humans, I would be stuck in the dark, with no hope in sight. The people in my life have shown up for me time and time again, and in this story they showed up at a time when I needed them most. I was in a hopeless state, losing faith, forgetting who I was, what I've worked for, and what I wanted.

The dark times can be consuming, especially when you have lost the ability to see the positive. During these experiences, you may want to tell everyone to fuck off, mainly those who are trying to get you back to being yourself. It's like the sadness feels good, because at least there is some sort of feeling at all. This is not a safe place to be, but it's the place I was in.

Sometimes, you need the extra help from the people who love you, to remind you who you are. While I was in this space, I had friends who listened to me cry, made me laugh, and friends who would text me lists of things that were beautiful in my life. Looking back, I am glad I got those messages as texts because to view the words in writing was impactful. It allowed me to physically see all the things I've accomplished, which helped me return to a space of gratitude.

Suddenly there was a shift in perspective. Now, let me just say it didn't happen overnight, but I eventually settled into a good place. I began to recall all the amazing things I've done in my life that not only made my life beautiful, but also made me a badass queen.

Yes my marriage ended, but my life is filled with great things. I have a career and a stable job. I have a home that is heated and warm for the winter. I have food in my refrigerator that I am able to buy for myself. I have friends and family who love me. I have my health and my intellect. I have my passion and my drive. I have a life that's worth living.

It didn't have to be this good for me. I should have been dead, or in jail, or institutionalized for the rest of eternity. That was where my life was headed. But I turned it around. I put in the work to change my circumstances from negative to positive. I made choices that would better my future. And I have been successful.

"Yes, thank you, more please," is a mantra that I began to repeat.

This was me saying YES to life. It was me honoring what I already had and what I have already accomplished up to this point. It was me expressing how thankful I was for my current reality. It was me identifying that more good is always on the way. As long as I can see the positive, and let go of the negative, I can be open to welcome more.

Affirmation
I am serene.
I am grateful.
I am rooted in the present moment.

Letting go takes time. It doesn't happen in a moment. Creating space for yourself to heal is essential, and staying positive in that process is vital. Trusting that everything is aligning for your future, while also being grateful in the moment, is what helps you to continue forward, especially when things get difficult.

In my own practice, gratitude keeps me centered and continuously takes me from projection to presence. The use of affirmations brings the focus from a negative thought to a positive thought, or from the future back to the present moment. It's within the space of gratitude that you are able to align with truth. The brain loves to trick you into delusional, or untrue thoughts, that can make you question your reality or your self-worth. When you can see the truth of all the good that already exists in your life, all the good that you already are, you can connect to all the amazing things you have. This, in turn, will multiply the positive energy that comes back to you.

Journal prompt:

1. *Create a gratitude list. This can be a continuous list that you add to each day, or you can make a new list each day. Add at least three things that you are grateful for in your current life.*
2. *Create an affirmation focused on gratitude.*

Example: Today I am grateful for my life. Yes, thank you, more please.

Section Five
"I See."

The Vision: Alignment of Heart & Mind.

Affirmation

I align with the belief of pure worthiness.

I embrace the courage to walk into the unknown.

I stay true to the vision of my created future.

It is so.

Intuition (noun)

In·tu·i·tion

   a: the power or faculty of attaining to direct knowledge or cognition without evident rational thought and inference

   b: immediate apprehension or cognition

   c: quick and ready insight

Now that you've had the opportunity to find a true connection with yourself through self-knowledge, understanding the power of your mind, and embracing the space of your heart, it's time to develop a clear vision of what you want your life to look like.

You have the ability to tap into the sense of *knowing* what's best for you. This is your intuition.

I'm sure you've experienced a time in your life when you ignored a feeling because your mind talked yourself out of it, telling you that it's just anxiety, or simply ignoring the gut feelings in general. I have, on multiple occasions, talked myself out of my intuitive feelings and all it got me was repeated patterns, emotional discomfort, and stuck in the same circle of choices. This is what I like to call the *lesson loop*. When you ignore your intuitive feelings, you get trapped in a loop of continuous experiences, until you are finally able to learn the lesson and move the fuck on.

The thing about listening to your intuition is, if you tend to ignore it, it's harder to hear. The more you begin to trust your intuition, the more messages you will receive. So in this part of your journey, I invite you to tap into your own inner knowing, and truly allow yourself to listen and hear what it's telling you. It is in this space of connection that you can focus your vision.

There are times you may struggle with second guessing your intuitive feelings, getting caught up in the "what ifs" cycle. When this happens, sit with the feelings, quiet the mind with self-regulation tools, and use affirmations for clarity. This refocuses your thoughts and aligns the mind with the heart.

I always do my best to honor my intuition by listening carefully and making choices that match my intentions and aspirations. The goal is to walk through fear and self-doubt, *knowing that the only way to change the cycle is to choose differently and embrace the unknown.*

When I am led by my internal instincts, a.k.a intuition, I am able to fully trust myself with true confidence. It's in this space where you are connected to your power, your words, and your ability to create your own reality.

Chapter 25: Focus

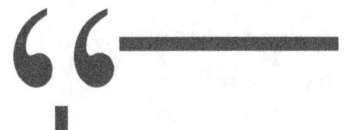

Affirmation

I am focused.
I am motivated.
I am confident.

I embody the courage to fully step into
my personal power.

I am successful.
I am passionate.
I am driven.

I am the creator of my desired reality.

It is so.

Focus (noun)

fo·cus

> **a:** a center of activity, attraction, or attention
>
> **b:** a point of concentration
>
> **c:** directed attention : emphasis

When crafting an intentional affirmation, it is most effective when you have a specific focus. This focus is ultimately your vision. But sometimes the focus is blurry.

Clarity of the vision is essential. When my vision isn't stable, it's typically because I'm having a hard time focusing on what it is I'm seeking to manifest. Sometimes my visions would come in clear waves, finding clarity in the moment, only to back track hours or days later because of my overthinking mind. This distorted my focus and often caused a lot of internal confusion.

Refocusing the mind with specific affirmations will help keep the focus on what it is you are working towards. It's a continuous reminder of your goals, dreams and desires, especially when the brain decides to come at you with fearful, doubtful thoughts.

Focus is how you sift through the lies and come to a point of clarity. It's in this space where you can find the words to help you along the way. When starting your personal process, you may not believe the things you are saying and that's okay. This is the action of connecting to your vision. The more you speak it, the more you'll believe it.

When you have clarity of intention,
the universe conspires with you to
make it happen.
- Fabienne Frederickson

In the summer 2024, during a Wim Hof breathwork session, I had an extremely emotional experience. I was struggling to find clarity with the ongoing attachment to my ex-husband, a whole year after our initial separation. I was filled with fear of the unknown, even though my intuition continuously (for years) was telling me it wasn't right to continue the relationship.

I remember this event as if it was just yesterday. It was a hot summer day in August and we were about two months into trying to make things work (again). The summer was chaotic. I was teetering between being comfortable in the familiar routine and constant anxiety that I was just prolonging the inevitable.

If nothing changes, then nothing changes. If I were to continue the course I was on, I would end up with the same results as before. Heartbreak, dysfunction, and turmoil. This revelation has occurred to me previously, but usually my fearful mind would convince me otherwise. But at this time, in this space of awareness, I could not deny what I already knew to be true.

During the summer prior, I started attending weekly breathwork and ice bath sessions to help calm my mind and body. I was having such a visceral reaction to my divorce and needed to try something new to help me in my healing process. This was a saving grace for me. I found peace, calmness, resilience, and most of all support from like minded people, most who were going through similar experiences.

When I arrived on this day, it was the first time I attended a session all summer. I knew I needed to be in a space of healing to help me gain a clear focus of what I needed to do to continue the path to my desired life. I was eager to get there. I knew in my heart that I was going to have a breakthrough of some sort, and to be honest I was desperate for it.

Going into the session, I could already feel myself coming to a breaking point. I was mentally drained. My heart was exhausted. My brain couldn't understand why I was continuing to live in insanity, repeating the same thing again and again.

I began to cry during the breathwork that day. This was not the typical experience for me. I've witnessed other people having this type of reaction, and was always a little jealous of their ability to release trapped feelings that needed to escape. I guess it was my turn. As I was going through the emotional release, my mind started to become clear and I kept hearing the phrase, *consistent clarity.*

I knew what the message meant. I needed to connect with continuous clarity. Clarity that wasn't interrupted by my thoughts. Clarity that came from my heart. Clarity that was undeniable.

Definition of Consistent Clarity
a: continuous clarity, unblocked by illusion
and overthinking.
b: to consistently think in a clear cut manner,
free from uncertainty.

This was a moment of enlightenment, where the agony became great enough and my soul was ready to let go and move on. This was me finally being able to fully connect to my intuition. The message gave me the strength to continue forward with focus, ultimately allowing me to realign with my vision.

At this time, I brought my focus back to my intentions and decided that it was time to get back on track. Once my mind was clear, the universe opened doors and gave me the strength to release the past, and the courage to move forward into the future.

Affirmation
I am grateful for my experience & lessons.
I am focused on my intentions & dreams.
I have faith in the process of creation.

The vision of your creation is amplified by consistent clarity and focus.

A key point in the process is to remember to focus on exactly what you want, not what you are currently lacking. Connect to the energy you wish you to attract into your life. Remember the power of positive thinking. You are what you think and imagine to be true. Change the narrative. Focus, feel, and believe. Eventually it will become reality.

Along the way, don't forget the practice of detachment. While focusing on your vision, sometimes you cannot see what specific result will be best for you. Therefore, it's important to be open to the possibility of receiving it in a slightly different way.

As we continue down this road, it's vital to bring the focus back to the concepts of gratitude and presence. It's within these practices that you can see the journey is always perfect, right here in the present moment. It may take time to get to where you want to be, but the way there is filled with joy, love, and the lessons that are necessary to endure in order to achieve your goals.

Journal prompt:

1. *What is your vision? Be as clear as possible.*
2. *What techniques can you use to declutter the mind?*
3. *How can you keep the focus on your vision?*
4. *Create an affirmation to cultivate a clear vision.*

Example: I let go of racing thoughts. I connect to clarity and truth, in this moment.

Chapter 26: Alignment & Balance

Affirmation

*I am open to encompassing balance,
allowing my path to evolve
without resistance.*

*I have trust in the universe,
knowing that all is progressing in
divine timing.*

*I am aligned with the energy of
this moment,
connected to a space of peace & harmony.*

It is so.

Alignment (noun)

align·ment

> **a:** the act of aligning or state of being aligned
>
> **b:** to be in or come into precise adjustment or correct relative position

To be aligned is such a deep concept. When I looked up the exact definition, it says to bring into "a line," which implies a straight, ongoing line that continues in the same direction. By this definition, the concept of alignment seems to be urging people to stay on one track. This does not resonate with me.

Humans are such complex beings. It is almost impossible to fit anyone into one specific box and have them stay in that box for an entire lifetime. People are constantly changing, adapting and growing. People are also made of energy, endlessly flowing. Everyone has different sides of their personalities that exist, that may not align with other aspects of themselves. That is the duality of energy that exists in every human, the yin and yang, the masculine and feminine. Everyone possesses it, and by this theory perfect "a line ment" cannot exist. That is why alignment, in my practice, is about balance.

I struggled with the duality of my personality for a long time. I have two completely opposing sides to myself that I can step into at any given moment. The free spirit and the over organized planner. This was hard to understand. I went through times of feeling bipolar, or just plain crazy. I felt like I didn't know who I was, and that one of the aspects could be the "fake me." It wasn't until I started to explore the journey of self, that I finally began to understand duality.

Spiritual practices and extensive self-study played a huge role in the knowledge I gained about myself, my energy, and my personality. When viewing alignment as a balance of self, I began to understand that I needed to accept and honor both sides of me. This is why the *perfect fit* is so difficult for people to find within their lives. There is no "one size fits all," therefore, there cannot be just one answer. The way to find inner alignment is to find a balance, a place where you can honor yourself wholly and truly.

When I am off balance, or not in alignment, my physical body will react. This is my body letting me know that I need to find equilibrium by honoring myself. It took me years to be able to identify what my body was telling me. This is the mind-body connection. When you have the ability to tune into the physical body, you can begin to understand how it's affected by your mind. For me, this shows up as anxiety. When a feeling is triggered by my mind, it attacks my body with an intense feeling of panic. I will have physical reactions, a racing heart, sweating, or a sinking feeling in my stomach. I can experience this often, especially in times of self-doubt or fear. However, I've been able to identify the feelings as my old thinking patterns trying to throw me out of alignment.

Since human beings aren't symmetrical or perfect, it's okay to be out of alignment. The number one thing I needed to learn in my process was to not be so hard on myself, and to let go of the idea of perfection, by continuously practicing self-love. The idea is to learn new reactions. So if you find yourself in a state of misalignment, and need to regulate in order to bring yourself back into balance, this is when you utilize what you've learned to achieve equilibrium thus far.

Again, humans cannot be perfect, and if anyone claims to be they're lying. Your first thoughts may always be the same, but it's what you do with those thoughts that actually matters.

Serenity is the tranquil balance
of the heart and mind.
- Harold W. Becker

The way I honor alignment of my duality is to allow myself to express whatever energy I'm in at the moment. I'm allowed to be free spirited and type A organized at the same time! The way I honor this is by doing things and participating in activities that allow me to be both. I travel often, which honors my need for freedom, but I do it in the most organized, OCD way, which honors my craving for security and stability.

In 2022, I began to explore travelling on my own. Up to this point, I travelled but only with my ex-husband. I am grateful for the places we visited together because it opened my very small world to the experience of exploration, and the curiosity to see new places. Before entering recovery, I didn't go anywhere. I was usually stuck in a five mile radius of my house, living the same day, over and over. This introduction really fed my soul and developed a passion for adventure.

My first solo trip was to Costa Rica in February 2022. I was meeting a friend there for my very first yoga retreat. I had to navigate getting there on my own because we both lived in different states and she was attending earlier than I was. I remember being nervous and anxious about how to get from the airport to the middle of the jungle with no one but myself to guide me.

The trip that's most notable for me was a yoga retreat in the Mayan Riviera, in Mexico, in February of 2024. By this time, I was officially divorced and felt incapable of completely managing travel without the verbal and emotional support of someone else.

I remember arriving at the airport three hours early. After having a speedy experience through TSA, I found my gate with two hours to spare. I sat down and began to get riddled with anxiety. This was not the first time that I flew by myself, and definitely not the first time that I solo traveled to a retreat. But at that moment, I felt like a child who needed help because, "I didn't know what I was doing." It was like an attack of impostor syndrome. I knew I needed to regulate before getting on the plane, so I turned to my practice.

I automatically began repeating a mantra in my head, "I am an adult. I have done this before." I repeated this over and over again until I was able to remind myself that I was completely capable of traveling by myself. I am not that insecure child that I used to be, I am an adult and I had successfully completed this same experience before, so this time would not be different.

After I was able to re-align with who the fuck I am, I continued on my journey with ease, grace and confidence.

Affirmation
I am courageous; strong & secure.
I am love; connected & balanced.
I am abundant; joyous & free.

I believe that the most important part of alignment is harmonizing your thoughts, words and actions. *Are you speaking and acting with the same energetic vibration? Are you backing up your words with the steps you need to take, in order to create those words into real life scenarios?*

Balance and alignment may come with uncomfortable feelings and fears. If you remind yourself of who you are, while also referencing past experiences, you can regulate and stay true to all aspects of self, even in moments of doubt.

It's easy to feel balanced and aligned when you are regulated (i.e. on a yoga mat or in times when everything is going right). The practice of affirmations can help you learn how to keep this continuity in words and actions when life decides to show up unexpectedly.

This is the balance.

You can lean into all sides of yourself by honoring your different facets with the choices you make. You can be more than one thing at one time. Celebrate your process by honoring the practice of self-love, especially in times where you may be falling short. Continue to use personal affirmations to bring yourself into alignment whenever you are feeling off balance.

Journal prompts:

1. *What are some dual aspects of your personality that you can identify?*
2. *How can you honor all aspects of you to find balance and alignment within yourself?*
3. *Create an affirmation to honor who you are, exactly as you are, in this moment.*

Example: I am beautiful. I am worthy. I am capable.

Chapter 27: Be Mindful
(Of Your Triggers)

Affirmation

*I honor myself by tuning into acceptance,
aligning my heart & spirit with truth.*

*I courageously walk through my triggers,
facing my fears, pain & discomfort.*

*I actively practice self-love,
remembering to embrace the things
I can control.*

It is so.

Humility (noun)
hu·mil·i·ty

    a: freedom from pride or arrogance
    b: the quality or state of being humble

There is a theory in spirituality that your soul is here to learn a lesson. The lesson will continue to show up, acting as a mirror to the things you need to mend within yourself, until it's finally received and healed.

Triggers are activators of this recurring *lesson loop*. They usually cause an intense, sometimes negative, emotional reaction. They really shouldn't be avoided because you are the only person who is responsible for your triggers. To avoid this responsibility would be to avoid learning the lessons of your lifetime. This was a daunting reality for me. However, the recognition was a necessary part of the journey, to manifest peace and personal power.

When I first began this process I was able to manifest things into my reality with a great deal of confidence. But, throughout the journey, I was met with unexpected challenges that led me down the road to where I am now. The unforeseen circumstances created a life path that asked me to step fully into my power by revealing the recurring lesson of attachment.

A major trigger is change, which is simply a challenge to your attachment to the past. When triggered by change, most people will react by trying to control everything and everyone around them. This is a common reaction because, as I've expressed, it creates a sense of safety. When you try to control people, places or things, the end result is usually disappointment or even pain. Pain is a great motivator. Sometimes it's what I need to finally be willing to make changes. But the truth is, it doesn't have to be that way.

To learn how to deal with triggers in a healthy way, you first must face those triggers. You have a choice. Avoid your triggers and change nothing, or, face your triggers and grow. Remember, *if nothing changes, nothing changes*. If you hide from your triggers they will have a hold on you forever.

I'll be the first to admit, this journey may come with moments of regression. Awareness of triggers can at times be unbearable. But that's the nature of awareness with no action. To take action against your triggers, you first must be aware, find acceptance, and then connect to humility, which will help you achieve the peace you seek within yourself.

Humility is all about letting go of the ego. The ego keeps you sick. It blocks you from seeing reality by keeping you stuck in the delusions of the mind. Affirmations increase humility because the practice itself is the act of letting go of ego. You tune into what you need to let go of and ask for what you desire in return. It really is another form of asking for help.

> *Life is a series of natural and*
> *spontaneous changes.*
> *Don't resist them; that only creates sorrow.*
> *Let reality be reality.*
> *Let things flow naturally forward in whatever way they like.*
> - Lao Tzu

My story comes with many triggers. Change. Self-doubt. Lack of control. Rejection. Just to name a few.

Change is inevitable. It can't be avoided. It is the only constant that truly exists in this world. Change has to be accepted and has to be faced. I could never hide from this trigger. I had no choice but to face it, especially during my divorce.

Self-doubt comes up often in my life. This trigger makes me feel unworthy, less than, or not good enough. But if I were to give into self-doubt, I would never have the ability to take chances. The risks I have taken in my life have led me to such amazing places. If I hid from self-doubt, I'd never have the opportunity to grow. I face this head on almost every day. Never more than when I was in school, searching for a job, and writing this book.

Lack of control is a major trigger. Attempting control is a "safety net," but also an illusion. I don't have control over anything; unless it is me, myself, and I. I can't hide from this truth. I don't have control over things, especially things that will trigger me. I can, however, control my reactions. My reactions to people. My reactions to situations. And most importantly my reactions to my triggers. I have to face this every single day because every day I am exposed to possible triggers that remind me of my inability to control things that are outside of me.

Rejection is bound to happen. It really can't be avoided. It isn't possible for every person to win or be chosen all the time, every day, for their entire life. It's triggering but it's reality. I had to face this trigger on multiple occasions, especially post divorce when dealing with dating and a breakup.

All of this realization and acceptance was an inside job. I had to learn to let go. Let go of attachment, and let go of the resistance to change. I had to become humble, identify trigger patterns, find acceptance, and become willing to make adjustments in order to cultivate inner peace.

This is where affirmations came into play. I use affirmations to call forth the courage and confidence to release my ego, face my triggers, and make choices that align the future with my truest desires.

The reality is, all of my triggers come back to the same ongoing issue (*cough cough*, life lesson). What does change, doubt, control, and rejection all have in common? My need for emotional safety. This is why I would often get attached to people. Being wanted by others gave me purpose, which in turn made me feel "safe."

Post-divorce, I was extremely triggered. I got involved with a new guy, ignoring all the red flags that were basically slapping me in the face. This was definitely a pattern.

When the relationship ended, all of my triggers were out in the open. I had to face yet another change in my life. I had to face more rejection which led to more self-doubt. All while accepting that everything that was happening was out of my control.

This was a big reality check. A big piece of humble pie. Avoidance and denial would never be the answer. The pattern of attachment was becoming undeniable. The answer was to face everything and allow myself to heal.

And I did. I used affirmations daily to increase my sense of self-worth. It took a *long* three months of self-love to find myself in a state of peace and contentment. But like I said, this journey can come with setbacks.

Along the way, I had a frustrating experience. One that I'm sure many can relate to. Awareness of my triggers has brought me to a place of understanding the motives behind my behaviors. But, even after doing the work, I can still find myself acting out on old patterns of thinking, usually triggered by a mindset of lack.

Shortly after the break-up, as I was going through my process of re-establishing my inner peace and self-love, I found myself reaching out via text. I told myself the sole purpose of the text was to bring clarity to a specific situation that occurred during the break-up. I convinced myself there was no motive for validation. But I think you already know, that wasn't completely true.

Ultimately this interaction left me feeling regretful. The response was short and vague, leaving me disappointed and feeling silly as hell.

This would usually send me into a tailspin. However, instead of beating myself up about the whole thing, I acknowledged that it was just another opportunity to practice self-awareness, and another reference point to make better decisions in the future.

Yes, this choice was based on a triggered feeling of loneliness but even with that, I didn't need to allow myself to become more triggered by the outcome. I found acceptance in the moment and moved the fuck on. That's growth!

I used to put a lot of my self-worth on how people act and the choices they make. I took it personally every time. The reality is that if people can't understand and express their own emotions, there's no way they can have compassion and understanding for others. It has nothing to do with who I am. I cannot take on responsibility for other people's actions. This is another false perception of control.

The mantra I began to use during this time is credited to Mel Robbins and *The Let Them Theory*. *Let him* not validate me and my feelings. *Let him* act like I'm a stranger. *Let me* continue to do the work and learn how to validate myself.

I can't control people. I can't control situations. I can't control outcomes.

I can control the way I see things. I can control the way I react. I can forgive myself, and others, for the past. I can find acceptance and embrace the unknown.

Embracing my triggers, and a consistent affirmation practice, helped me to lessen my reactions, find acceptance in what's in my control, and continues to guide me in making better choices.

Affirmation
I am safe to face myself.
I am safe to heal & grow.
I am safe to love & thrive.

You cannot rush healing. Believe me I have tried. Slowing down and sitting with your triggers can help you decipher the lessons at hand. It'll help you face them, understand them, feel them, and eventually heal them. Exposing yourself to your most provoking triggers can, in fact, help you practice this healing process.

Remember, you are the only person responsible for your own happiness. No one else has the power to do that for you. True joy is an inside job. People can trigger your own insecurities, especially when things don't go your way, but you have the power to change your reactions.

Be more forgiving and compassionate with yourself and others. Be the healer of your own wounds. Accept the lack of control over people, places and things. This is peace! Facing your triggers relinquishes the power they have over you. This gives you freedom. The energy of true peace and freedom, opens the pathway to creation.

You are worthy.

Journal prompt:

1. *What triggers are you currently observing in your life?*
2. *Are you living in ego?*
3. *How can you connect to humility in these situations to find freedom?*
4. *Create an affirmation to face your triggers and prepare yourself to heal and grow.*

Example: I see myself as I am, honoring the good and honoring what needs work. I gently walk through my challenges, ready and willing to heal and grow.

Chapter 28: Self–Validation

"

Affirmation

I am lovingly connected to the warmth of my heart.

I am abundantly aligned with the truth of my worth.

*I am brilliantly aware of the beauty of
my wholeness.*

It is so.

"

Validate (verb)

val·i·date

: to recognize, establish, or illustrate the worthiness or legitimacy of

Let me just start by saying, I'm an *expert* on the subject of self-validation, not because I'm perfect and healed, but because I live this practice every single day. I'm still learning, I'm still practicing, and sometimes, I'm still struggling.

Let's recap.

First, self-honesty and acceptance are so important when building a self-validation practice. Affirming yourself is the essence of self-love, which begins with honesty, self-awareness, and acceptance of the present moment. Within this acceptance, you are able to see the things that need to be adjusted, and cultivate the resilience to gradually and ease-fully make changes.

In this process you have become aware of learned behaviors and beliefs that may not be serving you and your highest calling. The awareness of these behavior patterns doesn't always make it easier to accept. Most times it makes it harder, because you are no longer naive to your reactions. Having self-knowledge enables the need for changes, which allows the space for you to let go and grow.

Remember, it is your choice to make changes in your life. You get to choose to forgive the past. You choose to let go of self-doubt. You choose to retrain your brain to release old thinking to embrace an optimistic view.

Redirection of thoughts is practiced through positive self-talk and affirmations. It is okay if you experience the same initial reactions at first, because eventually you'll have the ability to redirect the thought and act accordingly. Initial reactions are habitual and it takes time to let go of old patterns, so it's important to be gentle and kind to yourself in this process.

This transformation of thinking will take continuous commitment of opening the mind and shifting perspectives. Once you are willing to take this action, new routines will begin to develop, bringing you closer to a new way of living.

Within this space of change, your faith and trust will begin to increase, resulting in a connection to love, patience and gratitude. Here is where the focus becomes clear. You take responsibility for your life and your future. You then connect to true inner peace, and allow yourself to manifest your desired reality with grace and ease.

Throughout this process you will face challenges. The question then arises; *Can you walk through the fires of change and allow yourself to alchemize and transform, or do you stay stuck in your old ways of thinking and behaving, destined to repeat the same lessons again and again?*

Affirming yourself with positive self-talk will always help you stay vigilant. There will be times of great independence and times of great fall backs. Each time, you are learning something new and becoming better for the next experience. Each time, you are building strength and confidence to move forward and continue growing. The growth is the proof of this practice working in your life. Take a moment to look back at how far you've come. This is, in truth, a practice of self-validation.

When you become comfortable with uncertainty,
infinite possibilities open up in your life
- Eckhart Tolle

Self-validation means to choose me, to make my own choices, and to be confident in myself. During the process of untangling my past, I began to see the moments of freedom that I had already experienced throughout my journey. It is so important to identify these glimmering moments. Seeing my success and growth in my process helped me see that I have, in fact, been practicing this concept the entire time.

I can and I will.

The first point of identification is my recovery as a whole. After years of painful lessons, I made a conscious decision to adopt a healthy lifestyle, change behaviors, and begin doing the inner work. This built the foundation for all the things discussed and practiced within the pages of this book.

I am capable of doing hard things.

Another indication of self-validation is earning a masters in education. I had to release the doubt of others and believe in myself, and my goals, to make a decision based on my wants and needs. If you remember back to earlier chapters, I was met with a lot of fear and concern. But, I walked through that fear and enrolled regardless of all the pessimistic predictions that were occurring.

I am so grateful that in that moment I was able to step into my power. I've been so blessed in the development of my career. The hidden blessing is the fact that I now have a reference point to look back on, anytime I have to face the doubt and fear of other people.

I love myself, wholly and truly.

Another reference point testimony is the healing journey I experienced during and after my divorce. It's ironic that this ended up giving me so much clarity. It truly was a major breaking point that helped me step into my power. All my life I have struggled with being indecisive. There was always a feeling of impending doom behind making major choices, especially when it came to relationships. I have learned that when I stay in situations out of fear, I'm finding comfort in the perceived known outcomes of familiarity, and not allowing myself the space to grow.

So how did I release my ultimate pattern of attachment and codependency? I used affirmations to let go of my fear of the unknown. I made a decision to reconnect to my faith, and fully fall in love with myself, with the use of positive self-talk.

I am safe to heal.

The final reference point is this book. It truly played a huge role in my process of healing. It has evolved so much since the very first manuscript. Each life lesson, each moment of pain and triumph, has helped develop the pages in your hands.

The process of writing not only freed me from myself, it also allowed me to step into myself. Free from judgment. Free from self-doubt. Free from limiting beliefs. Each step of the way I learned how to reconnect to confidence and self-assurance. This pushed me to complete my goal and achieve my dream of becoming a published author.

I honor my own self-worth.

Each experience serves as a reminder that no matter what, everything has always been okay. Each experience I have endured has given me an opportunity to heal different facets of my being. Each experience has revealed patterns that needed adjusting. Each experience allowed me to face triggers and build resiliency.

Affirmations gave me the ability to keep going through each unexpected turn, leading me to an amazing place of healing. This journey brought me to a space of peace, and as you've learned, the key to manifestation is the cultivation of inner peace. Peace gives me the opportunity to match the energy I want to attract into my life on a daily basis. Within this energy I can manifest endless opportunities, ultimately creating the life I truly desire.

Through it all, I've built confidence within myself using the power of positive thinking and self-affirming words. This practice has given me the strength to choose peace, to choose happiness, to choose self-love, and choose me. And yes, all these things are choices.

Most of all, this healing journey helped me learn how to validate myself.

Actress, and self-love advocate, Julia Roberts, once said, "The space they left, the moments they dismissed you, the times they made you feel invisible—they were all silent gifts in disguise. Because in their absence, you found yourself. You learned to appreciate your own worth, to stand tall without needing anyone else to confirm your value. You built a life that is full, rich, and complete—not because of them, but because of you."

This quote hits home for me. I read this and I see my own journey of self-validation. I am responsible for my own healing. I am responsible for my own actions. I am responsible for using my life experiences as lessons to learn and grow. My power comes from within, not from anything, or anyone, outside of me.

It is an ongoing process. Affirmations enforce validation, which enforces belief in self. It can be difficult, but after some time, it becomes more natural. With continuous effort, I have been able to step into my own power, knowing that everything I want is within my reach, as long as I stay positive and believe in myself.

Affirmation
I call in faith & trust.
I call in confidence & courage.
I call in validation of self.

This journey has led me to a place of connection, faith, and self-love. It has helped me manifest the strength to trust the power of my own choices, find clarity, and accomplish great things, like finishing this book.

Today, maybe not all day but every day, I know that my life is beautiful. Self-validation is freedom from the mental cage of lack. It is the state of pure love, courage, and trust in your path. Some days you may need to, as Taylor Swift puts it, "Fake it till you make it (and I did!)." This *is* meeting the energy of the universe. This is matching the energy you want to receive. Eventually it won't be fake. Eventually you'll believe in yourself, and become aligned with your ultimate vision.

You are the healer and creator of your own reality. You harness the energy you want to attract by staying positive. Remind yourself daily that all is well. All is aligning perfectly in divine timing. And, you are safe within yourself.

Observe, reflect, let go, forgive. Continue to show up. Continue to do the work. Continue to free yourself from things that hold you back. Continuing the journey, no matter what, is an empowering freedom that everyone deserves to experience.

Allowance is the key to change.
Change is the key to freedom.
Freedom is the path to transformation.
Transformation is the path to peace.
Peace is the key to creating the life you desire.
-C.M.S.

Journal prompt:

1. *Where do you see glimmers of hope in your life, indicating your growth in this process?*
2. *How are you expressing your own freedom to choose?*
3. *Create an affirmation that is focused on validating yourself.*

Example: I am confident. I can make difficult decisions.
(I am _____. I can _____.)

Chapter 29: Visualization

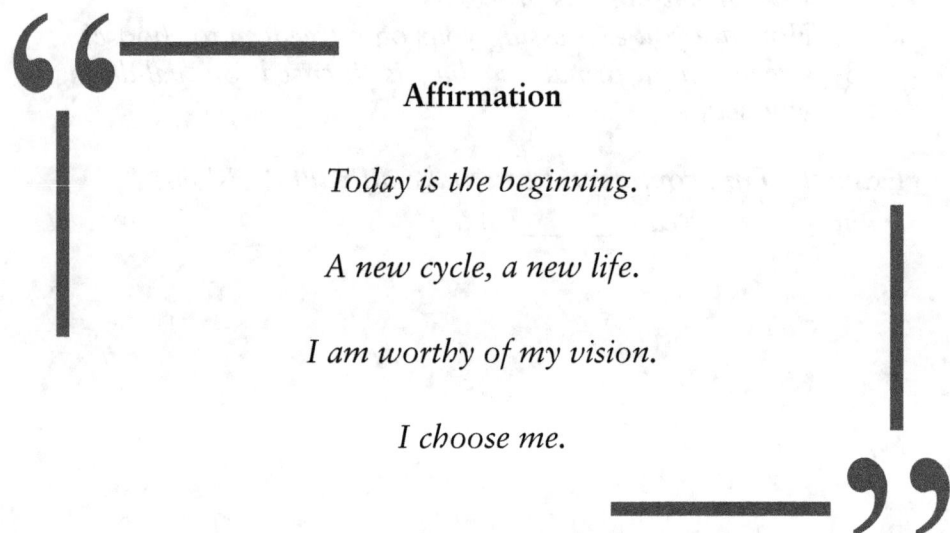

Affirmation

Today is the beginning.

A new cycle, a new life.

I am worthy of my vision.

I choose me.

Vision (noun)

vi·sion

   a: the act or power of seeing : sight
   b: something seen in the mind, a dream, or trance
   c: a thought, concept, or object formed by the imagination

Now that you have practiced the ability to validate yourself with the use of your words, and find your connection to inner peace, it's time to take it to the next level; visualizing your ideal future, decided by your own intentions and goals. Remember, visualization is a great tool when creating. Seeing things as if they already exist, is another way to attract that same energy into your world.

The two questions I like to ask myself are; *What is your vision? What are you trying to create?* Throughout this book the focus was on achieving self-knowledge, connecting to the heart, and stepping into the power of self. It's now the point of your process where you are able to truly connect to your intentions. Once you know what it is you want, it is time to speak it and visualize it into existence.

> *A spirit with a vision,*
> *is a dream with a mission.*
> - Neil Peart

My journey has been filled with manifestations that were material as well as mental and emotional. Looking back, I now see that all the things that have transpired needed to occur in the exact ways they did, to help bring me closer to where I wanted to be. The destination is not final, but I have clear goals and aspirations for the future and will continue to take the steps to achieve the life of my wildest dreams.

Each experience I went through has expanded my knowledge of self. I've fostered growth in ways that cannot be attained any other way but to live it. Because of the belief that all has transpired to elevate my existence in this lifetime, it is important to once again connect to detachment of specific outcomes. That may seem confusing, especially since I am asking you to begin visualizing what it is you want to create for yourself, but this concept of visualization is a connection to how the vision makes you feel.

The connection to *feeling* is what attracts the energy into existence. This is the same idea as connecting to the heartspace. The feeling raises the vibration of your energy, which you already know attracts the same energy from the universe. This is the secret to manifestation. When you get tripped up on specific outcomes, it blocks the energy from creating the best opportunity for you. That is why it is important to let go of expectations and focus on the feeling you desire to achieve from the creation of your vision. In this space, the energy will flow seamlessly. In this space, you are able to choose yourself, and your goals, everyday. Choosing you is your new super power, your own validation, your own voice. Stand in your power and tap into the creative energy that exists within you.

I don't always know what's best for me. I can only see what's right in front of me and develop perspectives and decisions based on what's in my sight. But if I open my mind to the understanding that the unknown is filled with unlimited potential, it is clear that when I fixate on only what I currently see, I am doing myself a dis-service.

In my experience, I've had moments of clear visions that manifested quickly and completely. Other times my vision was created within time and looked slightly different. I have also had situations where the vision would not come to fruition.

From this I have found that the universe has three answers to all the things you ask for; *yes, not yet, or there's something better.*

It's up to you to discern what is happening within each of your manifestations. All "yeses" will simply flow into existence seamlessly. The "not yets" will come with patience and time, and most likely, not look exactly as you planned. When the answer is "there is something better," you will be met with resistance and challenges at every turn. Practicing the law of detachment will help energy to flow and allow you to find acceptance in the answers that are being given to you.

You can't know what is ahead for certain. So, you cannot know for certain what grand plans are the right ones. Aligning with faith will help guide you to a place of acceptance and surrender. It'll encourage you to let go of outcomes and trust that all will be well, even if it isn't what you thought it would be. It will be better than you could even imagine because what is meant for you will always find you at the perfect divine moment.

Affirmation
I am free from stress & worry.
I am connected to peace & calm.
I am aligned with high vibrational energy.

Trust the process my friends. That is the simplest but most difficult thing to do. Some days are easy. Some days are harder than others. Some days are just about showing up. Some days are for acknowledging the small wins and being grateful for the experiences. Nothing is permanent and feelings will pass. When things get hard, and they will, stick to the belief that you have within yourself.

Release the urge to control and force outcomes. Have faith in the fact that what is meant for you will always come when it is supposed to. Continue the work. Your efforts never go unnoticed and will bring you closer to where you are supposed to be, even if it looks different than expected.

Let go of your past mistakes, have hope in your beautiful future, and fall into the space of peace. It is here that you can be present for the journey. Take it all in. Learn all the lessons. Experience all the feelings. Make your own choices. Change your mind if you choose to.

Throughout this book I've shared my personal way of writing affirmations but remember *this is YOUR practice. Write in your own way. Write in a way that will align with your vision. Write in a way to help build you up. Write in a way that will help you manifest your goals.*

There is no right or wrong in your timeline. To truly validate yourself, is to love and honor each and every part of your story. Keep dreaming. Keep taking the next step. And always remember, what you think, you create.

Stay confident. Speak to yourself kindly. Voice positivity into the world every chance you get. You are the creator of your reality, so make it the vision you see in your mind and feel in your heart.

Journal prompts:

1. *What is your vision?*
2. *What are you creating?*
3. *List 3 steps that you can take to achieve this vision.*
4. *Which of the 3 steps can you start right now?*
5. *Is there any resistance or challenges that you may need to take note of?*
6. *Create a specific affirmation to enhance the power behind your vision. Set aside five minutes a day to practice a "visualization" meditation focusing on seeing your vision as if it already exists. In this meditation, I invite you to focus on how you feel. Connect to the heart space and the joy that you feel in your vision. This will attract the energy of joy into your life.*

Example: I am (insert vision here).

Section Six
"I Align."

Endings are New Beginnings

Affirmation

I am safe within myself, within this moment.

I am strong, I am confident, I am secure.

I release the need to be validated by others.

I have the power to support & love myself.

It is so.

Purpose (noun)

pur·pose

> **a:** something set up as an object or end to be attained : intention
> **b:** resolution, determination

Life is a never ending cycle of change, lessons, and growth. Each experience leads you to the next, and each "next" brings about more insight to your purpose.

Validating yourself with the use of affirmations will help bring you closer to the life that you strive for. It helps cultivate the power of inner peace. It helps bring a clear focus to your own unique intent.

This is why I still use, and will continue to use, this practice every single day.

> *What you hope, you will eventually believe.*
> *What you believe you will eventually know.*
> *What you know, you will eventually create.*
> *What you create, you will eventually experience.*
> *What you experience, you will*
> *eventually express.*
> *What you express, you will eventually become.*
> *This is the formula for all of life.*
> - Neale Donald Walsch

Connecting to the power of my words has enhanced my life so deeply and pushed me to become the person I am today. For this, I am grateful. I have come to see that everyone has the ability to become creators, if you choose to release negativity, and embrace the power that resides within your being; your vibration, your energy, your thoughts, and your words.

The process of writing this book was in itself a practice of self-validation. It was a lesson that needed to be learned. It was an experience that needed to be had. It was a project that brought light to my purpose. Throughout the process, it was utterly obvious that this book wasn't just meant to help others. It was also created to enhance my own healing journey. The expansion of the writing within these pages changed overtime as I continued to learn my lessons, identify patterns, and release old behaviors. I saved every version of this book just to be able to go back and witness the evolution all over again.

While cultivating your own affirmations I urge you to keep everything. Keep all your journals. It's within your past writing that you will have concrete evidence of your own growth within the process. The development of your words and intentions will be proof of this practice moving you forward into a space of trust, faith, and belief.

Find your connection to the power of your words by simply beginning. Begin again each and every day. Remain vigilant and never give up on yourself. If you feel you've failed, just start again. You deserve all the joy and happiness that exists in this world. Once you realize the truth in those words, nothing will be able to hold you back. You will continue to take action until you have met your goal, and when you meet that goal, a new one will be on the horizon. If you fall down, take a moment to lick your wounds and then get the fuck up.

This lifetime is yours to create.

Stay in your power and manifest the future you seek, because it's there for you to own.

Chapter 30: "I Am. I Feel. I Affirm. I Love. I See. I Align."

Affirmation

*I connect to a calming energy,
feeling safe & secure within myself.*

*I embrace a peaceful presence,
aligning my vibration to the frequency of the universe.*

*I emanate loving vibes,
attracting the energy in which I want to receive into my
world.*

It is so.

In the following pages are the affirmations that I've used throughout this book. Please use them, share them, and make them your own. I invite you to utilize the knowledge you've learned to write your own affirmations, using the vibrational power of your words.

My hope is that these affirmations can be taken as guidelines, or as little pick me ups, whenever you need to reconnect to the power of your voice.

Remember, there is no right or wrong. Feel into the practice, stay in your heart, own your purpose, and morph your visions into reality.

Affirmation
I am Soft yet Stable.

I am Kind yet Strong.

I am Gentle yet Powerful as F*ck.

Affirmation
I free myself from the cage of my past,
accepting all that is & all that has transpired.

I acknowledge growth from my experiences,
moving through challenges to truly embrace
who I am.

I let go of self-judgment & regret,
finding the courage to practice forgiveness
& self-love.

It is so.

Affirmation

I am safe to be courageous.

I am safe to walk through fears.

I am safe to move through changes.

*I am safe to transform
into the strongest version of myself.*

Chapter 2: The Beginning *p. 6*

Affirmation

*I let go of expectations,
& allow myself to feel the energy of peace.*

*I welcome new possibilities,
& explore opportunities to practice growth.*

*I appreciate the process of healing,
& embrace the experiences of my journey.*

All is manifesting for me NOW.

Chapter 3: The Now *p. 11*

Affirmation
I am magnetic.

I am magical.

I am attracting aligned energy.

It is so.

Chapter 4: The Magic of Affirmations *p. 16*

Affirmation
I am confident.
I manifest & create my reality.

I am successful.
I have endless potential & possibilities in my life.

I am worthy.
I deserve all of my dreams & intentions.

I am. I am. I am.

Chapter 5: I Am *p. 23*

Affirmation
I am in tune with my language,
my personal vibration & source of connection.

I am aligned with self-expression,
tapping into confidence & positive vibration.

My words are my power & my sovereignty,
the link to higher energetic frequency.

It is innately mine.

Chapter 6: Words Are Power *p. 29*

Affirmation
I feel into the essence of who I am,
fully secure within myself.

I feel into the space of hope & faith,
self-assured within the present moment.

I feel into the power that resides
within my being,
trusting that all is being manifested.

It is so.

Section 2: "I Feel." You're Personal Power
(You are personal power) *p. 35*

Affirmation
Tuning into the body.
I am rooted & secure.

Tuning into the mind.
I am peaceful & clear.

Tuning into the heart.
I am light & love.

Tuning into the breath.
I am alive & free.

Chapter 7: Breath, Rest, Repeat *p. 37*

Affirmation
I am confident within the understanding of truth.

I am secure within the freedom of honesty.

I am faithfully connected to my words,
expressing responsibility through
the language of authenticity .

It is so.

Chapter 8: Honesty *p. 49*

Affirmation

I am tuned in to awareness of self,
acknowledging areas of potential growth.

I am aligned with the healing powers
of the universe,
connected to the energy that flows within.

I am honoring all aspects of me,
embracing my journey with love & kindness.

It is so.

Chapter 9: Self-Awareness *p. 55*

Affirmation

I accept myself truly & fully,
honoring & loving all parts of me.

I accept others wholly & respectfully,
witnessing through a lens of kindness
& compassion.

I accept the absence of control,
focusing on the things that are within my own power to adjust.

I shift into a space of ease,
believing that acceptance is calmness &
calmness is liberation.

It is so.

Chapter 10: Acceptance *p. 61*

Affirmation
I courageously walk through self-doubt,
connected to my confidence & self-assurance.

I align myself with the clarity of truth,
fully free to feel safe within my own journey.

I am brave & I am worthy.

It is so.

Chapter 11: Release Self-Doubt *p. 68*

Affirmation
I am released from the cage of resistance,
allowing myself to open the door to connection & hope.

I embrace the journey of transformation,
allowing myself to be in the energy of
peace & calm.

I align with trust in the unfolding,
stepping into a space of pure freedom to
choose me.

It is so.

Chapter 12: Unlocking Independence *p. 74*

Affirmation

I am home within myself;
affirmed, grounded, & strong.

I am free from obsession of the mind;
balanced, secured, & focused.

I am grateful for clarity in this moment;
centered, connected, & clear.

It is so.

Section 3: "I Affirm." The Mind. *p. 83*

Affirmation

I open my mind to endless possibilities,
ready to receive the gifts of the unknown.

I wholeheartedly embrace acceptance,
trusting all is unfolding for my highest potential.

I free myself from the fear of change,
having confidence & hope for all that is to come.

It is so.

Chapter 13: Opening Your Mind *p. 85*

Affirmation
I shift my perspective,
seeing the truth of distorted thinking.

I am aware of my thoughts,
freeing my mind of old patterns & beliefs.

I release the illusion of control,
trusting the path to endless possibilities.

It is so.

Chapter 14: Shifting Perspectives *p. 91*

Affirmation
I allow myself to let go,
creating space for faith & love.

I embrace the beauty of my life,
opening my world to an abundance of gratitude.

I attract the energy I am seeking to receive,
calling in unlimited opportunities.

I choose peace. I choose calm. I choose me.

It is so.

Chapter 15: Choice *p. 98*

Affirmation
*I am willing to put in the work to achieve
my intentions.*

I am worthy of living the life of my true desires.

I am able to do hard things.

It is so.

Chapter 16: Willingness *p. 105*

Affirmation:
*I release the urge to force,
freeing myself to move gracefully.*

*I step into a state of allowance,
effortlessly connecting to the flow of life.*

*I embrace gentle action,
balancing effort, patience & easeful change.*

*I align with positivity & passion,
truly knowing that no matter the outcome,
all is well.*

It is so.

Chapter 17: Gentle Action *p. 111*

Affirmation
*I let go of worried thoughts,
allowing myself to stay present on the path.*

*I am aligned with what I can control,
understanding that there are things I cannot.*

*I am regulated within the body & mind,
staying grounded in confidence & hope.*

I am safe. I am focused. I am committed.

It is so.

Chapter 18: Commitment *p. 118*

Affirmation
I am safe, in this home which is my heart.

I am safe in this place & in this time.

All is well.

Section 4: "I Love." The Heart. *p. 125*

Affirmation
I am one with the space of my heart,
aligned & connected to my emotions.

I am worthy of compassion & kindness,
free from insecurity & doubt.

I am innately deserving of an abundance of joy,
finding gratitude in the love that exists within me & around me.

It is so.

Chapter 19: Connection *p. 127*

Affirmation
I am calm,
having trust in myself, the universe & my path.

I am peace,
having acceptance in each moment, experience & life lesson.

I am serene,
having faith that all is well, beautiful & joyful.

Being within the presence of this moment,
It is so.

Chapter 20: Faith & Trust *p. 135*

Affirmation
I surrender my obsession with the past
& the future.

I forgive myself for mis-takes
& repeated patterns.

I connect to happiness & joy
in the here & now.

It is so.

Chapter 21: Surrender *p. 143*

Affirmation
I release fear.
I release insecurity.
I release second guessing myself.

I call in faith.
I call in confidence.
I call in love & trust in myself.

I connect to peace.
I connect to forgiveness.
I connect compassion for myself.

It is so.

Chapter 22: Self-Love *p. 150*

Affirmation

I open my heart to the peace of patience.

I open my mind to the calmness of contentment.

I open myself to the tranquility of trust.

It is so.

Chapter 23: Patience *p. 157*

Affirmation

I see the light within the darkness.

I see the love in each moment.

I see the beauty in all those around me.

I am grateful.

It is so.

Chapter 24: Gratitude *p. 164*

Affirmation
I align with the belief of pure worthiness.

I embrace the courage to walk into the unknown.

I stay true to the vision of my created future.

It is so.

Section 5: "I See." The Vision: Alignment
of Heart & Mind. *p. 171*

Affirmation
I am focused.
I am motivated.
I am confident.

*I embody the courage to fully step into
my personal power.*

I am successful.
I am passionate.
I am driven.

I am the creator of my desired reality.

It is so.

Chapter 25: Focus *p. 174*

Affirmation
I am open to encompassing balance,
allowing my path to evolve without resistance.

I have trust in the universe,
knowing that all is progressing in divine timing.

I am aligned with the energy of this moment,
connected to a space of peace & harmony.

It is so.

Chapter 26: Alignment & Balance *p. 180*

Affirmation
I honor myself by tuning into acceptance,
aligning my heart & spirit with truth.

I courageously walk through my triggers,
facing my fears, pain & discomfort.

I actively practice self-love,
remembering to embrace the things I can control.

It is so.

Chapter 27: Be Mindful (Of Your Triggers) *p. 186*

Affirmation
*I am lovingly connected to the warmth
of my heart.*

*I am abundantly aligned with the truth
of my worth.*

I am brilliantly aware of the beauty of my wholeness.

It is so.

Chapter 28: Self Validation *p. 194*

Affirmation
Today is the beginning.

A new cycle, a new life.

I am worthy of my vision.

I choose me.

Chapter 29: Visualization *p. 202*

Affirmation
I am safe within myself, within this moment.

I am strong, I am confident, I am secure.

I release the need to be validated by others.

I have the power to support & love myself.

It is so.

Section 6: "I Align." Endings Are New Beginnings. *p. 209*

Affirmation
I connect to a calming energy,
feeling safe & secure within myself.

I embrace a peaceful presence,
aligning my vibration to the frequency
of the universe.

I emanate loving vibes,
attracting the energy in which I want to receive into my world.

It is so.

Chapter 30: I Am. I Feel. I Affirm. I Love. I See. I Align. *p. 212*

Acknowledgments

Be Extraordinary Publishing
Lawrence Pabelloren Tuazon & Kerry Fisher

Be Extraordinary Publishing is a visionary publishing house dedicated to empowering authors, thought leaders, and changemakers to transform their ideas and stories into impactful works that inspire, inform, and influence the world. Founded on the principles of excellence, creativity, and authenticity, the company provides a comprehensive, author-focused approach to the publishing journey.

At its core, Be Extraordinary Publishing is more than just a publishing house—it's a partner in creating legacies. The mission is to guide writers through every stage of the book creation process, from conceptualization and manuscript development to publication and beyond. The goal is not just to produce books but to elevate authors as recognized voices in their fields, fostering enduring trust and loyalty with readers.

Be Extraordinary Publishing isn't just about producing books—it's about helping authors shape the extraordinary futures they envision for themselves and their readers.

Editor

Mary Carpenter is a freelance editor and writer, specializing in non-fiction and poetry. Based in Brooklyn, she has helped to tell and tailor numerous narratives over her decade career.

Mary's dedication to this book has been a true blessing. This work would not have reached its current form without her unwavering efforts and the meticulous care she invested at every stage of the journey.

Long Island Writers Guild

To the remarkable group of individuals who gather on the fourth Monday of every month at The Next Chapter in Huntington, NY: Thank you for truly hearing me, seeing me, and inspiring me to share my stories. Each of you has played a vital role in my journey of improvement, growth, and the deepening of my passion. Your invaluable feedback, suggestions, and edits have all contributed to the creation of this book. I am deeply grateful for your support!

The Humans Behind the Quotes

Abraham Hicks

Abraham Hicks refers to the teachings of Esther Hicks, who channels a group of non-physical entities called "Abraham." Along with her late husband Jerry, she promotes the Law of Attraction, emphasizing that positive thinking and alignment with desires can shape one's reality and lead to fulfillment. They have authored several books and conducted workshops, influencing many in the self-help and personal development fields.

Bob Proctor

Bob Proctor was a Canadian author, speaker, and personal development expert known for his work on the Law of Attraction and positive thinking. Born on July 5, 1934, he authored books like *You Were Born Rich* and *The ABCs of Success*, focusing on personal growth, success, and financial freedom. Proctor gained widespread recognition from the documentary *The Secret*. He held seminars globally, teaching individuals to unlock their potential and transform their mindset for a fulfilling life. Proctor passed away on February 3, 2022, leaving a lasting legacy in personal development.

Bryant McGill

Bryant McGill is an American author, speaker, and social entrepreneur known for his work on personal development and social issues. His book *Simple Reminders* focuses on mindfulness, positivity, and living a meaningful life. McGill empowers individuals to create positive change and shares inspirational messages on social media. He also advocates for social causes like environmental sustainability and mental health awareness, blending practical advice with motivational insights to inspire personal growth and authenticity.

Buddah

Buddha, born Siddhartha Gautama, was an Indian prince who founded Buddhism. After encountering suffering, old age, illness, and death, he sought enlightenment. Through ascetic practices and meditation under the Bodhi tree, he achieved enlightenment and became known as the Buddha, or "the Enlightened One." He taught the Four Noble Truths and the Eightfold Path, focusing on understanding suffering, mindfulness, compassion, and liberation from samsara. His teachings continue to inspire millions globally.

Catherine Pulsifer

Catherine Pulsifer is an author, motivational speaker, and poet known for her inspirational writings on personal development, positivity, and the power of words. She focuses on themes like resilience, gratitude, and self-improvement, offering simple, relatable messages that encourage individuals to pursue their goals and embrace change. Her motivational pieces and poetry are widely shared, inspiring readers seeking encouragement in their lives.

Dalai Lama

The Dalai Lama, Tenzin Gyatso, is the 14th spiritual leader of Tibetan Buddhism and the head of the Tibetan government-in-exile. Born on July 6, 1935, in Tibet, he became the spiritual and political leader at age 15. Known for his teachings on compassion, nonviolence, and inner peace, he advocates for Tibetan autonomy and promotes dialogue with China. Awarded the Nobel Peace Prize in 1989, he travels globally, sharing his insights on Buddhism, ethics, and mindfulness through books and talks, earning respect worldwide for his emphasis on compassion and interconnectedness.

David G. Allen

David G. Allen is an author and speaker known for his book *Getting Things Done: The Art of Stress-Free Productivity*, published in 2001. He developed the GTD (Getting Things Done) methodology, which helps individuals and organizations organize tasks to boost productivity and reduce stress. Allen's approach focuses on capturing, clarifying, organizing, reviewing, and engaging with tasks in a focused manner. He also conducts workshops on productivity and goal setting, making a significant impact on personal development and efficiency.

David Crow

David Crow is the author of *The Pale-Faced Lie*, a memoir about growing up as a Native American in a family with a complex history. The book explores themes of identity, culture, and resilience, focusing on Crow's personal challenges and relationships, particularly with his father. It also reflects on the broader social issues faced by Indigenous communities, offering candid insights into Native American identity and heritage. The memoir has been praised for its poignant storytelling and deep cultural perspective.

Deepak Chopra

Deepak Chopra is an Indian-American author, speaker, and alternative medicine advocate, known for his work in spirituality, health, and wellness. Born on October 22, 1946, in New Delhi, India, Chopra integrates Western medicine with Eastern philosophy. He has authored best-selling books like *The Seven Spiritual Laws of Success* and *Ageless Body, Timeless Mind*. His teachings emphasize the connection between mind, body, and spirit, promoting meditation, consciousness, and holistic health. Chopra is a leading figure in the mindfulness and wellness movement, inspiring millions to explore personal growth and well-being.

Dr. Shanti Shanti Kaur

Dr. Shanti Shanti Kaur is a respected teacher, healer, and author known for her work in the fields of yoga, meditation, and holistic healing. She is particularly associated with Kundalini Yoga and has taught extensively in these practices, focusing on personal transformation and spiritual growth.

In addition to her teachings, Dr. Shanti Shanti Kaur has written about the benefits of yoga and meditation for mental and physical health. Her work often emphasizes the importance of mindfulness, self-awareness, and the integration of mind, body, and spirit.

Eckhart Tolle

Eckhart Tolle is a German-born spiritual teacher and author, best known for his book *The Power of Now*, which emphasizes living in the present moment and the role of consciousness in personal transformation. His teachings focus on presence, the nature of the mind, and transcending ego-based identities. In addition to *The Power of Now*, he has written *A New Earth* and *Stillness Speaks*. Tolle is a sought-after speaker, leading workshops and retreats worldwide, inspiring millions through his teachings on spirituality and mindfulness.

Fabienne Frederickson

Fabienne Frederickson is the founder of Boldheart, a coaching company that helps entrepreneurs and business owners grow their businesses while maintaining a balanced personal life. Known for her expertise in marketing, sales, and personal development, she offers programs and workshops that combine practical strategies with mindset shifts. Frederickson is also an author and speaker, sharing insights on entrepreneurship, confidence, and aligning business practices with personal values.

George Bernard Shaw

George Bernard Shaw was an Irish playwright, critic, and social activist, born on July 26, 1856, in Dublin. Known for his sharp wit and social commentary, he wrote over 60 plays, including *Pygmalion, Saint Joan*, and *Man and Superman*. A leading figure in the Fabian Society, Shaw advocated for social reform, women's rights, and education.

His works, often using humor and satire to challenge societal norms, earned him the Nobel Prize in Literature in 1925. Shaw's influence continues in discussions on social justice and the role of art in society. He passed away on November 2, 1950.

Harold W. Becker

Harold W. Becker is an author, speaker, and founder of the Love Foundation, a non-profit dedicated to promoting love and compassion worldwide. Known for his work on the transformative power of love, Becker encourages individuals to cultivate love in their lives and communities. He has written books such as *Unconditional Love: An Unlimited Way of Being* and *The Love Foundation: A Journey of a Thousand Miles*. Through his foundation, he organizes events and workshops to inspire positive change through love.

Lao Tzu

Lao Tzu, also known as Laozi, was an ancient Chinese philosopher and the founder of Taoism, believed to have lived around the 6th century BCE. He is best known for writing the *Tao Te Ching* (Daodejing), a key Taoist text that explores the Tao (the Way) and principles of harmony, simplicity, and naturalness. Lao Tzu's teachings emphasize living in harmony with the natural order, advocating for humility, compassion, and moderation. His philosophy has deeply influenced Chinese culture and continues to inspire people worldwide, especially with its focus on balance and interconnectedness.

Mahatma Gandhi

Mahatma Gandhi, born Mohandas Karamchand Gandhi on October 2, 1869, was an Indian leader who played a key role in India's independence struggle through his philosophy of nonviolent resistance, or "Satyagraha." His commitment to civil disobedience, social justice, and equality made him a global icon for civil rights. Gandhi worked for causes such as poverty eradication, women's rights, and the upliftment of marginalized communities. India gained independence in 1947, but Gandhi was assassinated on January 30, 1948. His legacy continues to inspire movements for peace and justice worldwide.

Mark Victor Hansen

Mark Victor Hansen is an American motivational speaker, author, and entrepreneur, best known as the co-creator of the *Chicken Soup for the Soul* series. Born on January 8, 1948, he has authored numerous books on personal development, inspiration, and success. *The Chicken Soup for the Soul* series, co-created with Jack Canfield, features uplifting stories and motivational essays, selling millions of copies worldwide and inspiring spin-offs on various themes. Hansen is also a sought-after speaker on entrepreneurship, motivation, and success, making a lasting impact on the self-help genre.

Neale Donald Walsch

Neale Donald Walsch is an American author and speaker, best known for his *Conversations with God* series, which began in 1995. The books present a dialogue between Walsch and the voice of God, exploring themes of personal growth, spirituality, and the meaning of life. Translated into multiple languages, the series has resonated with many readers worldwide. In addition to his books, Walsch conducts workshops and speaks globally, promoting love, compassion, and spiritual exploration to inspire deeper connections with oneself and others.

Neil Peart

Neil Peart was a Canadian musician and author, best known as the drummer and primary lyricist for the rock band Rush. Born on September 12, 1952, in Hamilton, Ontario, Peart joined Rush in 1974, contributing to their distinctive sound with his exceptional drumming and thought-provoking lyrics. His lyrics often explored themes like individualism, time, and the human experience. In addition to his work with Rush, Peart authored several books on drumming, music, and travel. Widely regarded as one of the greatest drummers in rock history, he passed away on January 7, 2020, leaving a lasting legacy in music.

Paulo Coelho

Paulo Coelho is a Brazilian author best known for his international bestseller *The Alchemist*, a modern classic. Born on August 24, 1947, in Rio de Janeiro, Coelho has written numerous novels and works on spirituality and personal growth. His writing, which explores themes of self-discovery, destiny, and the pursuit of dreams, is known for its philosophical reflections and narrative simplicity. In addition to *The Alchemist*, notable works include *Brida, The Valkyries,* and *Eleven Minutes.* Coelho is one of the most translated authors globally, with his books available in over 80 languages, and his personal journey has deeply influenced his work.

Peter McWilliams

Peter McWilliams was an American author, publisher, and advocate known for his writings on self-help, personal development, and drug policy reform. Born on August 5, 1949, he gained popularity for books like *How to Survive the Loss of a Love*, which offers guidance on grief, and for his advocacy of medical marijuana. McWilliams' candid, humorous writing resonated with readers and made him a prominent figure in discussions about drug policy and personal freedom. He passed away on June 16, 2000, leaving behind a lasting legacy through his influential works.

Rumi

Rumi, born Jalal ad-Din Muhammad Rumi on September 30, 1207, was a 13th-century Persian poet, Islamic scholar, and Sufi mystic. He is best known for his spiritual poetry, exploring themes of love, the divine, and the soul's journey. His most famous work, the *Masnavi*, serves as a spiritual guide. Rumi's poetry transcends cultural and religious boundaries, emphasizing love and the connection between the individual and the divine. His works, translated into many languages, continue to inspire readers worldwide. Rumi passed away on December 17, 1273, leaving a lasting legacy through his teachings and poetry.

Sam Cooke

Sam Cooke was an influential American singer, songwriter, and entrepreneur, often hailed as a pioneer of soul music. Born on January 22, 1931, in Clarksdale, Mississippi, he transitioned from gospel to pop and R&B, with hits like "You Send Me," "A Change Is Gonna Come," "Wonderful World," and "Cupid." Cooke's music, addressing themes of love and social justice, made him a key figure in the civil rights movement. Tragically, he was shot and killed on December 11, 1964, at age 33. Despite his brief career, his profound impact on music and culture endures, solidifying him as one of the greatest vocalists of his time.

Satsuki Shibuya

Satsuki Shibuya is an intuitive artist and spiritual guide whose practice is deeply rooted in spirituality, with each creation emerging from her profound connection to the unseen. Based in Los Angeles, Shibuya's journey began with a background in music and design, but a pivotal period of illness deepened her spiritual insights and redirected her focus toward the healing arts. www.satsukishibuya.com

Thich Nhat Hanh

Thich Nhat Hanh was a Vietnamese Zen Buddhist monk, teacher, and peace activist known for his teachings on mindfulness and compassion. He founded the Plum Village Tradition and authored influential books like *The Miracle of Mindfulness* and *Being Peace*. A pioneer of engaged Buddhism, his work inspired millions worldwide. He passed away on January 22, 2022, leaving a lasting legacy of peace.

Yung Pueblo

Yung Pueblo, the pen name of Diego Perez, is a poet and writer known for his reflections on self-healing, mindfulness, and personal growth. He gained fame through impactful quotes on social media and books like *Inward* and *Clarity & Connection*, which blend poetry and prose to inspire emotional healing and self-discovery.

Meditation Resources

Dr. Joe Dispenza

Dr. Joe Dispenza is a neuroscientist, author, and speaker known for exploring the power of the mind in personal transformation. Through books like *Breaking the Habit of Being Yourself* and *Becoming Supernatural*, he teaches how changing thoughts and beliefs can improve health and well-being. Dispenza blends neuroscience, quantum physics, and ancient wisdom, using meditation and visualization as tools for transformation. He conducts workshops and retreats worldwide, inspiring people to break limiting patterns and tap into their mind's full potential. Learn more at www.drjoedispenza.com.

Tony Robbins

Tony Robbins is an American author, entrepreneur, and motivational speaker known for his best-selling books like *Awaken the Giant Within* and *Unlimited Power*. His high-energy seminars, such as "Unleash the Power Within," inspire individuals to achieve success in personal development, leadership, and finance. Robbins is also a philanthropist, supporting initiatives in health, education, and social justice. Through his work, he has empowered millions worldwide to transform their lives. Learn more at www.tonyrobbins.com.

Deepak Chopra

Deepak Chopra is an Indian-American author, speaker, and alternative medicine advocate known for his work in spirituality, health, and wellness. He has written numerous best-selling books, including "The Seven Spiritual Laws of Success," "Ageless Body, Timeless Mind," and "The Healing Self."

Chopra's teachings focus on the connection between mind, body, and spirit, emphasizing the importance of consciousness, meditation, and holistic health practices. He promotes the idea that individuals can achieve well-being and personal transformation through awareness and spiritual practices.

Through his website, Deepak Chopra shares resources, articles, and programs related to meditation, health, and spirituality. He is a prominent figure in the wellness movement and continues to inspire many people around the world with his insights and teachings. www. deepakchopra.com

Wim Hof

Wim Hof, also known as "The Iceman," is a Dutch athlete and wellness advocate famous for his ability to endure extreme cold and perform remarkable feats like running a marathon barefoot in the snow. He developed the "Wim Hof Method," combining breathing techniques, cold exposure, and mental focus to boost physical and mental performance. Hof claims his method can enhance immune function, health, and energy. Through books, workshops, and media appearances, he promotes this method for personal empowerment and well-being. Learn more at www.wimhofmethod.com.

Calm App

The Calm app is a popular tool for mental well-being, offering guided meditations, sleep stories, breathing exercises, and soothing music. Designed to reduce stress, improve sleep, and enhance mindfulness, it caters to both beginners and experienced users. Known for its user-friendly design and high-quality content, Calm helps users incorporate relaxation into daily life. Learn more at www.calm.com.

Headspace

Headspace is a meditation and mindfulness app offering guided sessions, sleep aids, and relaxation tools to reduce stress, improve focus, and support well-being. Known for its simple design and engaging content, it helps users build a more mindful lifestyle. Learn more at www.headspace.com.

More References

Alex, A. (2023, September 5). *What is inspired action and how does it work? (5 tips).* Manifest Like Whoa! https://manifestlikewhoa.com/inspired-action/

Aronson, J., Cohen, G., & Nail, P. R. (2019). Self-affirmation theory: An update and appraisal. In E. Harmon-Jones (Ed.), *Cognitive dissonance: Reexamining a pivotal theory in psychology* (2nd ed., pp. 159–174). American Psychological Association. https://doi.org/10.1037/0000135-008

Cascio CN, O'Donnell MB, Tinney FJ, Lieberman MD, Taylor SE, Strecher VJ, Falk EB. Self-affirmation activates brain systems associated with self-related processing and reward and is reinforced by future orientation. Soc Cogn Affect Neurosci. 2016 Apr;11(4):621-9. doi: 10.1093/scan/nsv136. Epub 2015 Nov 5. PMID: 26541373; PMCID: PMC4814782.

Complete guide to the 7 chakras: Symbols, effects & how to balance: Arhanta yoga blog. Arhanta Yoga Ashrams. (2024, November 13). https://www.arhantayoga.org/blog/7-chakras-introduction-energy-centers-effect/

Editors, Y. (2024, January 25). *What is pranayama?.* Yoga Journal. https://www.yogajournal.com/practice/beginners/how-to/pranayama/

Kim J, Kwon JH, Kim J, Kim EJ, Kim HE, Kyeong S, Kim JJ. The effects of positive or negative self-talk on the alteration of brain functional connectivity by performing cognitive tasks. Sci Rep. 2021 Jul 21;11(1):14873. doi: 10.1038/s41598-021-94328-9. PMID: 34290300; PMCID: PMC8295361.

Merriam-Webster. (n.d.). *America's most trusted dictionary.* Merriam-Webster. https://www.merriam-webster.com/

Oxford Learner's dictionaries | find definitions, translations, and grammar explanations at Oxford Learner's dictionaries. (n.d.). https://www.oxfordlearnersdictionaries.com/us/

Robbins, M. (2024). *The let them theory: A life-changing tool that millions of people can't stop talking about.* Hay House LLC.

Santos-Rosa FJ, Montero-Carretero C, Gómez-Landero LA, Torregrossa M, Cervelló E. Positive and negative spontaneous self-talk and performance in gymnastics: The role of contextual, personal and situational factors. PLoS One. 2022 Mar 24;17(3):e0265809. doi: 10.1371/journal.pone.0265809. PMID: 35325003; PMCID: PMC8947089.

More References

Srini Pillay, M. (2018, March 14). *Can you rewire your brain to get out of a rut? (yes you can...).* Harvard Health. https://www.health.harvard.edu/blog/rewire-brain-get-out-of-rut-2018030913253

Steele, C. M. (1997). A threat in the air: How stereotypes shape intellectual identity and performance. *American Psychologist, 52*(6), 613–629. https://doi.org/10.1037/0003-066X.52.6.613

TerKeurst, L. (2020). *Forgiving what you can't forget: Discover how to move on, make peace with painful memories, and create a life that's beautiful again.* Nelson Books.

Webb CE, Dennis NA. Memory for the usual: the influence of schemas on memory for non-schematic information in younger and older adults. Cogn Neuropsychol. 2020 Feb-Mar;37(1-2):58-74. doi: 10.1080/02643294.2019.1674798. Epub 2019 Oct 4. PMID: 31583953; PMCID: PMC8919503.

What is the astral body? Magickal Spot. (2024, January 23). https://magickalspot.com/astral-body/

What is the law of attraction & how does it work?. The Law Of Attraction. (2023, August 15). https://thelawofattraction.com/what-is-the-law-of-attraction/

About the Author

Caitlin Santomauro has a passion for health, wellness, and personal growth which was born from her own journey of transformation. She is a health educator, a certified yoga teacher, energy worker, and a somatic healer.

During her own healing journey, she discovered the life-changing power of affirmations to overcome challenges and reclaim her personal strength.

This experience inspired her to guide others in unlocking their inner power. Through recovery and spiritual practices, she gained profound insights into the connection between words, energy, and self-belief—insights that are the heart of her book, *The Language of Self-Affirmation: A Magical Practice of Manifesting Personal Power.*

She shares practical tools and inspiration to help readers harness the magical power of affirmations, manifest self-confidence, and create lives filled with joy, peace, and purpose.

Her work is a powerful guide for anyone ready to discover their potential and step into a life of true empowerment.

For more information and inspiration, follow Caitlin on Instagram; Manifesting_caitlin.